For to See the Elephant

A novel-in-verse

Elephant.

To be seen at Mr. Treadwell's Tavern until Monday evening October 15th, then positively to be removed.

THE ELEPHANT is not only the largest and most sagacious animal in the world, but from the peculiar manner in which it takes its food and drink of every kind, with its trunk, is acknowledged to be the greatest natural curiosity ever offered to the public. The one now offered, to the view of the curious, is a Female. She will draw the cork from a bottle, and with her trunk will manage it in such a manner, as to drink its contents. She is 15 years old, and measures upwards of 20 feet from the end of her trunk to that of her tail; 13 feet round the body, upwards of 8 feet high, and weighs more than 6000 pounds. Perhaps the present generation may never have an opportunity of seeing an ELEPHANT again, as this is the only one in America, and this perhaps is the last visit to this place.

Hours of exhibition from 9 in the morning until 6 in the evening.

Admittance, 25 cents for all over 12 years old—From that to 5 half price. No contracts will be made for whole families.

by Tammi J Truax

For to See the Elephant
© 2019 by Tammi Truax

Printed in the United States of America

Published by Piscataqua Press
32 Daniel St., Portsmouth, NH
03801

Newspaper clipping courtesy of The Portsmouth Athenaeum

www.ppressbooks.com

Publisher's Cataloging-in-Publication Data
Names: Truax, Tammi J., author
Title: For to See the Elephant / by Tammi J. Truax
Description: First trade paperback original edition. / Portsmouth,
NH: 2019. / Includes discussion questions.
Summary: The history of the first elephants to come to America,
told in verse.
Identifiers: ISBN 978-1-950381-05-0
Subjects: LCSH: Juvenile fiction / elephants / early American
history.
CYAC: Novels in verse. – Historical fiction. - Fiction.
Classification: LCC PZ7.5
FIC Tru
ATOS data: Book level 5.5, AR points 3, word count 22,330.

ISBN: 978-1-950381-05-0

Tammi Truax doesn't flinch from the harsh realities of a boy growing up in a time of slavery or in the lives of elephants forced to live away from their kind on another continent. But she also shows the beauty found by those who look close into the eye of an elephant, the love an animal and caretaker forge, the occasional kindness of strangers who can see beyond spectacle, and the brief freedom of leaving dusty roads to frolic in ponds.

Jeannine Atkins
author of *Borrowed Names: Poems about Laura Ingalls Wilder, Madam C.J. Walker, and Marie Curie and Their Daughters* and *Finding Wonders: Three Girls Who Changed Science*

The tenderness between a boy, William, and an elephant draws you in. The boy sees "all her beauty there/in her eye/ it look like/ a topaz marble...." He becomes her keeper. The travels of an elephant keeper and each of his charges is drawn almost entirely from historical fact. Truax turns documented history into verse narrative and binds the reader to the tragedy of her tale.

Terry Farish
author of *The Good Braider*

When I read this story in verse, I feel the return of a sacred quality in my bones for captive creatures. I feel the sad strangeness of the wondrous animals tended by slaves, on display as curiosities. I am encircled, as an elephant in the wild, by a greater understanding for their living sorrows.

Erine Leigh
10th Portsmouth (NH) Poet Laureate

Dedication

This book is dedicated to the elephants and their keepers at The Elephant Sanctuary in Hohenwald, Tennessee. You can visit them and donate at www.elephants.com.

Introduction

This is a historical novel-in-verse that is based on the history of the first two elephants that came to America. It is based on real people, animals and events, but is a work of fiction. The history of the first two elephants, and moreso their keepers, was poorly recorded and reliable documentation is scarce. I studied everything I could find on the subject and wrote these original and found poems. The found poems are taken from diaries, newspaper articles, advertisements, and songs of the period. More detail is provided in the author's notes at the end of the book.

A few words about the title of this book and elephant idioms

The title of this book, *For to See the Elephant*, were words written not by me, but by President George Washington, at the end of his second term in Philadelphia. A fastidious accountant, the president made a notation in his household account book on November 16, 1796 of the amount he had spent "for to see the elephant". While I don't think he coined the phrase I can find no earlier references to its use. But it would soon become a common phrase, and then an idiom, one that is sometimes called an Americanism.

There are a number of elephant idioms in the English language (an idiom is a word or phrase which means something different from its literal meaning), perhaps in every language. That is because the elephant has had a major influence on humans throughout history. To see the elephant (or its past tense, have seen the elephant), are American idioms that have become obsolete, and so people no longer know the original meaning. The history, like that of the elephants in early America, is rather sketchy and impossible now to determine with complete accuracy, but in the nineteenth century everybody in America understood what it meant and people of all ages would have used it.

It was based on the fact that the first elephants in America were so incredibly popular that people would go to great lengths to see one. It has been said that boys would steal from a loved one, and men would sell their valuable farm equipment to come up with the cash to see the elephant. People would also travel considerable distance to do so, at a time when travel was never easy. Within a few decades the phrase was used in reference to any time-consuming task or journey that took all of one's energy, money, or even their life. It came to be commonly used about sojourns west, especially to engage in mining or to service in a war. It meant that you had accomplished a life event that was grueling, and you had made it through to the other side, and now the experience was yours, something no one could take away from you, and that would stay with you forever, for better or worse. This story will take you on a sojourn to see the elephant.

There are a number of other old elephant idioms that are still commonly used. I have sprinkled a few of them throughout this story for you to find.

There is no creature among all the Beasts of the world which hath so great and ample demonstration of the power and wisedom of almighty God as the Elephant.

Edward Topsell

The Historie of Foure-Footed Beastes 1607

Captain Jacob Crowninshield
City of New York
May 1795

One must prepare properly.
In assembling my crew
for the *America's* next voyage
I found myself wanting.

A simple stop-over
at the New York City slave market
allowed me to acquire
a boy.

Paid a bit more than desired,
but he appears sturdy and able,
and didn't vex excessively
when parted from his mother.

Pray he takes well to the sea
for we disembark on the morrow.
I shall call him
William.

GAJA
AT LEAVING BENGAL, INDIA
OCTOBER 1795

My mahout was conflicted that day. I could tell. I could tell by the silent language of his body. Further, I could tell that he needed me to go where he was leading me, but that in his heart he did not really want me to go. I also knew I had been sold. I saw the transaction take place in the market where so many, many things were bought and sold, bought and sold, bought and sold. Where bargains were haggled, arguments were raised and settled, goods of all kinds were always moving, moving, moving. That is where I usually came in, helping to move the big things. But that day, someone, a stranger, had approached my mahout. They conversed for quite a while. My mahout had nothing to sell, but of course, my services.

The man, who was not Indian and dressed in an odd way, took great interest in me. He touched me on my shoulder and then my rump. Tentatively at first, like a little child might. That was fine, for a time, but he became more intrusive. He circled around close behind me, where I could not see him and I do not like that. Then he came around the other side and lifted my ear. Yes! Lifted it right up, and looked inside. I knew not why. Then, and this I did like, he looked me in the eye, right up close where I could see his and see it well. He was an inquisitive fellow, full of ideas and plans, and those seemed to involve me at the moment. I could smell him. It was a fairly foul smell, as most people put forth, but worse than usual. This man had a fishy and fleshy smell. I knew that he was a flesh eater, and thus found him threatening. There was a tinge of an alcohol scent which was not all that uncommon, but no sign at all of the spices that I liked to smell on people; my favorites being tamarind and turmeric, as those are redolent of my favorite foods. Also coriander and cardamom were almost always pungent on the skin of people I encountered. But not this foreigner. He stroked my trunk. It was a very forward gesture,

2

but it was not entirely disagreeable to me. It seemed friendly enough in intent, but I wrapped my appendage around my mahout's arm to show my own personal preference. My mahout leaned into my head, and I, into his.

The foreign man put his hands on his hips, and backed up a few steps. I hoped that meant he was going away. But he just seemed to be sizing me up. Looking me up and down, and my young mahout too, so that I began to feel protective. I made a very low, not too serious, growling sound, and my mahout gave me all of the settle down and be still commands using his lowest voice, which I of course, obeyed. The man bent down and forward in a submissive stance, placing his hands upon his knees. I was not fooled by the gesture, feeling no trust for him what so ever. He squinched his eyes half shut and peered at me. He was trying to look into my mouth. Of what need would a man have to see the inside of my mouth? I admit I considered in that moment snapping his head off, and I have at times over the years since, wondered how life would have been different if I had followed my first instinct. But I pride myself on being a peaceful pachyderm, and so chose a more civilized response. I had had enough of this nonsense and picked up my right foot and then set it down. Calmly but forcefully enough to let the mahout know how I felt. I was still but a baby, and had little patience for foolishness. My mahout gave me another settle down command, and the haggling resumed. I turned my head and waved my trunk into the breeze so that I could be soothed by more pleasant smells, and I communicated with another elephant some distance away who seemed to be having a more pleasant morning than I, and offered me some kind-hearted encouragement in return.

It was at that moment that I felt the surge of bad feelings flow through my mahout, his hand upon my leg, and turned back in alarm. The man had extracted a purse from deep within his waist coat, and was handing my mahout many rupees. More than I had ever seen exchanged. My mahout accepted them all and looked conflicted even then. To my great satisfaction the odd man turned about and began to walk away leaving the market place. But my mahout nudged my ankle with his foot, the command for me to march. Forward, to follow the man. I didn't like the suggestion, but since he was walking right along beside me, at my shoulder as usual, I did as he asked. I always had, and had always been fairly rewarded for doing so.

Soon I saw it; the sea. A great big beautiful thing. As I, like all of my others, enjoy water, I was quite happy to see it, and lumbered toward it without provocation. When we were close I was halted. That frustrated me. I wanted to go to the water. To bathe and play. I wanted to frolic in the abundance of it. But men, many more who looked like the foreigner we had followed, were yelling at each other with words that were not of a friendly sounding sort. We were brought abreast of a vessel, a big wooden one with many sails overhead. Its big sails snapping in the wind reminded me of elder elephant ears and I tried to read their messages, but could not. There was much conversing with my mahout, proud that he was being consulted by so many grown men. I did not like the feelings the situation was giving me but I was not afraid. Just nervous with uncertainty. I trusted that my mahout would take care of me as he always had.

I was given a meal, a decent one. As I chewed slowly and happily, the men were walking on and off the boat by way of a narrow plank bridge. It was not hard to determine that it could not hold me and so I was not concerned that that was their objective. Yet I knew they had an objective that involved me. It seemed to be getting me on board. Many men came to take a look at what was happening. They all seemed to have an opinion to share with the others, shamelessly flouting a false knowledge for not a one of them knew what it would take to get me on the boat.

I do not like bridges. No one with any good sense should. They are foolhardy. As are boats. A bridge to a boat is not something I would consider. Far more foolishness than I had ever been willing to tolerate before. The men began looking up. A large mechanical crane came into view. I was unfamiliar with such a machine. I swayed to convey my apprehension. Then I began to feel a bit sleepy and sluggish, having been fed something that dulled my senses. My

4

mahout came to the talking place, just in front of my left eye. I wrapped my trunk about his waist as I always did in tender moments. He stroked me softly and spoke to me in his lowest voice. Several sentences, that were soothing in their sound, but not thoroughly sincere. I sensed that he was promising me that everything was going to be just fine, and I simultaneously sensed that he was not at all sure that was true. Then he kicked me in my ankle, and led me to the crane. I knew that he needed me to obey. I never wanted to disappoint my mahout, and I knew if I did disobey, he would be humiliated in front of all the men gathered there, and I would not bring him such shame. My mahout had always been proud of me.

Straps were wrapped around my midsection, tightly. Then hooks were attached to the straps. Though feet had never left the ground before I was lifted up, and soon was sailing in the air not at all like a lovely winged creature. It was terrifying, and I cried out, but soon was lowered to the deck of the ship. With much maligning and maneuvering I was backed down a ramp into a hold in the dark belly of the boat that was already bouncing about on the water in a way I did not enjoy. I did my best to comply with all commands, even the most confusing ones, and did not retaliate when I was shoved and slapped.

Then the worst happened. Something I had not even considered might happen. My mahout, with just a glistening of tears in his little brown eyes, kissed me on the spot between the bumps in my forehead, said softly, "phir milenge", turned and ran away. Up and out of the darkness. The makeshift hold was closed and fortified by men on the other side.

I let out an trumpeting roar, one I knew he could hear as his little bare feet flew across the wharf in the opposite direction that I was headed. I was but a baby and had never been left alone before.

i've settled into this

being a deck hand

there are moments

few and far between

when it is nice

when i am above

and the sea is soft

and the sails are tight

and i pretend

im a bird in flight

returning home

to find

my mother

once

when we were at

the bay of benghal

a boy came aboard

a boy and his beast

i was more interested

in the boy

i have been around

only old men for so long

and the boy was brown

like me

but he ran away

i wish i'd thought of that

it seems he left

his big smelly beast

for me to tend

My dear brothers,
We take home a fine young
elephant
two years old, at $450.
It is almost as large
as a very large ox,
and I dare say
we shall get it home safe.
If so
it will bring at least $5000.
I suppose
you will laugh at this scheme,
but I do not mind,
will turn elephant driver.
It will be a great thing
to carry
the first elephant
to America.

your obedient servant,
J Crowninshield

Mayhap
it was a mistake.
Mayhap
I should have filled the hold
with the riches
commonly taken aboard
at India;
silks,
perfumes,
ivory,
spices,
pretty, aromatic goods.
This beast smells of hell.
Worst of all,
and most unsettling
is the sound.

I say with certainty
I've never heard
a sadder sound
than the cry of
The Elephant.

Adding to the misery
of the cries,
the beast thrusts itself
in rhythm with the rise
and fall of the sea,
against the pen

built to hold her.
A haunting,
            thumping
ever so sad sound.

I pray
that it holds
for it is only a length of chain
designed to yoke
Africans in transport
that tethers
her right foot.

I pray
that it holds
for the beast
could kill a man
with little effort.

I pray
perhaps
the gracious tidings
of Christmas time
will find their way
to the belly
of the *America*
and bless all souls
aboard this ship.

captain said

i'm to take care of

the Elephant

me

the smallest one here

captain said

i'm african

so i should know -

what that mean

captain said

get the beast

to calm down

and clean up

all her mess

captain aint said

how

ELEPHANT ON BOARD

The day begins with moderate breezes.

We have stopped at Saint Helena.

The beast remains below.

All of the men disembark employed in landing

23 sacks of coffee, pumpkins and cabbages,

some fresh fish, and greens for

the Elephant.

The men got several turtles and saw a large sea lion.

We are having trouble keeping water.

It drinks so much!

I've told the boy to hold her off.

I've a plan yet to try.

We have plenty of porter.

Perhaps as with men

alcohol will dull its senses

and make it sleep.

William
at sea
February 1796

first time

i climbed in the hold

i was scared

but i jus say

easy girl

i aint gonna hurt you

i give her

water and food

an i pat her

real slow like

an a course

i clean her mess

i go round back

where i know she

dont want no one

could kill me dead

but i rub her leg

where the chain be

i know chains hurt

i tell her

she dont have to

do that sad

back n forth dance

nor smash her head

no more

imma stay with her

in the hold

i make a bed

out of hay

in the corner

i lay down

she watch me

with one eye

but that night

she stop

banging her head

seems like

she never sleep

It exceeded my most
earnest expectations.
I was sitting in
The Bulls Head Tavern
enjoying some rabbit stew.
The Elephant
was tethered out front
on the great Broadway.
Droves of people came.
Two to strike a bargain.
A cattle driver named Bailey
had a bulging purse
having just sold his all
at the slaughter house,
when of a sudden
a Welsh man stood up, cried
*"Ten thousand dollars for
the Elephant."*
I was so pleased
I threw in the boy,
and a bottle of porter.

thought i'd always

be a deck hand

turns out

i'm a elephant hand

i got sold again

i hope to stay in this place

where my mother

might be

I'm counting on that negro

to take good care of

the Elephant.

He seems to be

doing his best.

Saw him teach her

to work the water pump.

She learned right quick.

How the people cheered!

All ages of people,

from all of places.

I find she needs

to be fed ever so much.

Eats more than any animal

I ever laid eyes upon.

It's costly, keeping her fed.

Though tis just greens, hay

and fresh water.

Ever so much water!
I don't care to pay
for her drinking porter,
but she does like it,
and the people like
to see her do it.

So we'll be walking
from city to city
going north for summer
all the way up
to the district of Maine.

Then south for winter.
Got to make my money back.
Just got to keep her alive
til I make my money back.

i'm called

the elephant

keeper

i like that

it is the job

of a man

not a boy

go from one town

to the next

folks pay to see

the Elephant

sometime we sleep

under the stars

sometime me and gaja

get put up in a barn

while the master

boards in a house

sometime he forget

to feed me

sometime i got to

steal a drink

out some cows teat

but i dont never

forget to feed

the Elephant

i'm

the elephant

keeper

Tonight she makes

her stage debut!

I have rented out

the Elephant

to the Philadelphia Theatre.

I'll have the boy

wash and oil her all up.

Not sure if I'll let the boy

take her on stage

or if I'll do it.

She seems to like the boy

much more than me.

The Elephant

Lately from India

and the first that was ever

upon this continent,

may be seen for a few days.

A place is filling up in Metropolis,

for his reception at the Panorama.

Price for grown persons

is half a dollar,

for child a quarter.

In size he surpasses

all other terrestrial creatures;

and by his intelligence,

he makes as near an approach to man

as matter can approach spirit.

I went off with Hannah Perabertons
to take the air in her carriage.
We walked under the covered market
to avoid wet pavements,
WD pointed to an alley
"there," said he, is kept
The Elephant.
I concluded to see it.

The innocent, good-natured
ugly beast was there,
it is indeed a curiosity
one-of-a-kind
never having been in this
part of the world before.

I could not help pitying
the poor creature
whom they keep
in constant agitation,
and often give it
rum or brandy to drink.

I think they will finish it 'ere long.

23

Ladies and Gentlemen!

Your generosity is sorely needed.

A portion of today's proceeds

will be distributed to the victims

of the great fire that recently

wrought great destruction upon

the good city of Savannah, Georgia.

The Elephant

will carry your coins

to those so struck by calamity.

Give generously!

Thank you, that is

right kind of you.

We had yesterday the funeral

of a young black born of African parents.

The appearance was pleasing to humanity.

All of them were clean and they were dressed

from common life up to the highest fashion.

We saw the plain homespun and the rich Indian

muslins and trail, so that they completely aped

the manners of the whites, and in happiness

seemed to surpass them.

Then this morning

I went to the market house to see

the Elephant.

The crowd of spectators forbade me

any but a superficial view.

He was six feet four, of large volume,

his skin black as tho' lately oiled.

A short hair was in every part,

but not sufficient for a covering.

His tail hung one third of his height,

but without any long hairs at the end.

He could not be persuaded to lie down.

The keeper repeatedly mounted him,

but he persisted in shaking him off.

Bread and hay were given him, he took

bread out of the pockets of spectators.

He also drank porter and drew his cork,

conveying the liquor

from his trunk into his throat.

His tusks were just to be seen

beyond the flesh, and it was said

had been broken. We say his

because of the common language.

It is a female. So I have seen

the Elephant.

Be it Known to All:
The ELEPHANT
according to the account
of the celebrated BUFFON,
is the most respected
animal in the world.
A sufficient proof that
there is not too much said
of the knowledge of this animal is,
that the proprietor having been absent
for ten weeks, the moment he arrived
and spoke to the keeper
the animal's knowledge
was beyond any doubt confirmed
by the cries he uttered,
til his friend came within reach of his trunk
with which he caressed him
to the astonishment of all.
He is only 4 years old,
and weighs about 8000. He measures

from the end of his trunk
to the tip of his tail
15 feet 8 inches.
He eats 130 weight a day, and
drinks all kinds of spirituous liquors.
He is so tame that he travels loose,
and has never attempted to hurt anyone.
A respected place is fitted up
adjoining the store of Mr. Bartlett,
for the reception of
those ladies and gentlemen
who may be pleased to view
the greatest natural curiosity
ever presented to the curious,
which is to be seen
from sunrise until sundown,
every day in the week.
The Elephant
having destroyed many papers of consequence,
it is recommended to visitors not to
come near him with such papers.
Admittance one quarter of a dollar
Children one eighth of a dollar

listen gaja-girl

i didnt know nothing

bout no elephant

fore you

lift that foot up now

there, there,

that good

now we be

traveling these roads

going to see folks

town after town

might as well

do the best we can

since we dont have

no dang choice no how

way i see it

we get a lot more

rewards for this work

than most other kinds

we both eating

and drinking good

i get a coin to keep

time to time

i like it better

walking like this

and you know

you do too

so lets put

our heads together

see if we can

make this life

not be so bad

for both of us now on

hows that sound

i promise ya one thing

nothing no way no how

ever get me

to take the whip to ya

mister say

it wont hurt you none

may not

on the outside

so when you hear

the whip crack

you do a trick

you get a treat

thats how

it will be

for you

and me

Some the time we have trouble

traveling the road.

Some the time

the Elephant

smells something to eat or drink

and she steps off.

More often the trouble is that

the Elephant

scares a horse.

Some horses spook easy.

I tell folks

I'm sorry for the trouble

but I'm not responsible

for they own spooky horse.

Then there is

the porter problem.

It's a good trick but she likes it

altogether too much.

And truth be told

I think the boy

been drinking porter too.

Thick as thieves, those two.

So, there's these things

to consider, remember,

if you want to buy

the Elephant.

i can tell

when gaja smell

fresh water

can see it in her

she flap her ears

and hole her trunk up

way before

any water in sight

then she walk

at a fast clip

and mister like that

we mos the time go slow

when we come

to the water

she tear off and

mister start to yelling

she stop and smell it

lookin for danger

she take a little taste

then a big one

then she spray herself

then, very slowly

she wade in

jus like the song

she clean herself

then plays awhile

takes a swim

under if she can

so whenever she bathe

i sing

that song for her

she like that

Wade in the water
Wade in the water, children

Wade in the water
God's gonna trouble the water

Who's that yonder dressed in blue?
Wade in the water
Must be the children that's coming through
God's gonna trouble the water, yeah

Wade in the water
Wade in the water, children
Wade in the water
And God's gonna trouble the water

today was real warm

and i was as dirty as

the Elephant

so when she found water

an i couldnt see any

white folks round

i pull off my clothes

an wade in the water

never seen gaja so happy

like near to drown me

that was a good time

yes it was

36

mister showed up

an he wasnt mad

til she throw dirt

all over herself

an we be

all dirty again

school student Patricia S.
Delaware
September 1799

What I Did On My Summer Vacation

I helped my parents.
I do the laundry;
washing, drying, folding
and some mending of my own.

I helped mother inside;
taking care of the baby,
setting up vegetables,
and churning butter.

Churning is my favorite.
On churning day I sing
the butter cake song
to my baby sister.

I helped father outside.
Taking care of Marigold, the lamb,
I don't like picking caterpillars
off the plants. Makes me cry.

We work like that
six days a week
but on Saturday night
we all have a bath.

On Sunday we go to church
and have a big dinner
with the cousins.
Everyone eats my butter.

The best Sunday of all
was in July.
After church, father took
all of us children

in the wagon, all the way
to Elmira, for to see

the Elephant.
This is real and true.
It has a long nose
called a trunk,
it uses the long nose
not just to smell.

It can pick things up,
and spray water
and make a loud noise
and pull a cork from a bottle.

I picked a flower
for her to smell.
She made a happy
little chirping sound.

And her boy smiled
as if it were his job
to smile for
the Elephant.

my voice has gone

an dried up

for yelling out all day

crowds was so big

but something else

happened in boston

down on the wharf

when we was sp'osed to be

buying greens and ale

i think he done it partly

to please

the Elephant

but mostly to please

his purse

everybody happy bout it

but me

going to be a lot more work

for me

and it spits

the mister bought

a dat burn monkey

and the mister

who wont call gaja nothing but

the Elephant

said the monkeys name

is little lord monboddo

if that

dont beat all

i jus dont know

what the devil do

Mister Welshaven Owen
Rhode Island
October 1800

The boy called William
is sickly.
Not sure what ails him
but he can't keep up.

I intend to leave him off
in the Federal City
as a barn boy
while I go south.

I made known to him
the slave catchers
that patrol the roads
routinely now,

and took his shoes.

The exclamations of the landlord

brought his wife in the room.

She curtsied, made many apologies

for the badness of the fire.

Added that her waiting man Bill

had run away, and having whipped

the other till his back was raw

she was willing to try

what gentle means would do.

A dinner of venison and a pint of Madeira

made me forget I had walked thirty miles

and it being little more than 4 o'clock,

I proceeded on my journey.

The vapors of a Spanish cigar

promoted cogitation, and I was

lamenting the inequalities in the world

when night overtook me.

I redoubled my pace
not without the apprehension that
I should have to seek
my lodgings in some tree,

to avoid the beasts
that prowled nightly in the woods,
but the moon, which rose
to direct me in my path,

alleviated my perturbation
and in another hour I descried
the blaze of a friendly fire
thru the casements of a log house.

Imaginings are worse
than real calamities.
The same being who sends trials
can also inspire fortitude.

The place I reached was Asheepo,
a hamlet consisting of three log houses,
and the inhabitants had collected
round a huge elephant.
I could not but admire

the docility of

the Elephant,

who in solemn majesty received

the gifts of the children

with his trunk.

But not so the monkey.

This man of Lord Mondobbo was inflamed

with rage at the boys and girls,

nor could the rebukes of his master

calm his fury.

I entered the log-house which accommodates travelers.

An old negro-man had squatted before the fire.

Well, old man, said I, *why don't you*

go out to look at

The Elephant?

Hie! He said, Massa, he calf.

The Elephant

came from Asia, the negro from Africa,

where he'd seen the same species,

of much greater magnitude.

There being only one bed in the house

I slept that night with the elephant driver.

Mr. Owen, a native of Wales,

carried a map of his travels in his pocket.

At noon, I was left to prosecute my journey alone.

The Elephant

would not travel without his dinner,

Mr. Owen halted under a pine tree

to feed the mute companion of his toils.

Mister Welsahven Owen
a southern state
Spring 1801

Bore da,

sir, I should very much like

to pay all of the damages,

and would very much like

to apologize again

for the unfortunate incident.

We travel from place to place

to bring people gladness at seeing

the Elephant,

and never before has anything

like this happened, I assure you.

The thing is, I'm sure you understand,

I can't stay awake every minute,

and I was asleep in your barn.

It would've been helpful if you'd told me

you'd a keg o' rum stored there.

Look at her nose!

She can smell anything.

48

God's honest truth sir,
she opened that keg herself
and drunk the whole thing.

Never seen her so soused!
Don't even know why she took to
tossing your property 'round
and made such a mess.
She knocked me down too,
never done that before.

She's always easy and amiable.
It was the liquor that done it.
She may be grieving for her keeper,
my boy William who I left behind
to recuperate his sick self.

As I said I'll make amends.
As much of a nuisance
as this has been I must tell you
sir, it could've been much worse.

That rum could've killed her,
then we'd have an entirely
different calamity to tend to,

she being of great value.

Might also have killed my monkey.

I'm not at all sure that he is well,

as he's quite sick this morning.

Additionally, my good man,

I must ask for a favor.

I'd be much obliged

if you'd see fit to refrain from

telling about what happened here

beyond this farm. I'll pay a bit extra.

Let us shake on it.

Then we'll be getting on our way.

I think it best if

the Elephant

walk this off, the best cure

for all overindulgences.

Bore da!

Came back to Washington City

to retrieve my hand, William.

He does seem to be faring well

and has grown tall as a man.

Still he seems awful thin.

Says it's on account of

not having enough to eat

and that his legs shriveled up

for want of walking.

No matter, we're taking him back.

I learned that I can't tour

the Elephant

on my own. And my word!

Were those two creatures

happy to see each other!

Even the mean little monkey

who can only be made happy

with candy or fruit or some such,

did a little dance at the reunion.

More Washington City wonder

is that yesterday, just before sundown

the President of these United States

came to see

the Elephant.

I do believe that Will and even

the Elephant

took pride in that.

I'll never forget it.

Nope, never will.

i'd been working with her

so long

to let me climb up on her

i tap her knee

to kneel down

and she do (but dont like to)

then I climb up

and finally today

she let me stay

i yelled for mister

he said only

it shouldnt have

take me so long

to get the ugly beast

to do that trick

i slid down

when he walk away

landed hard

on the dusty grass

got in front

of her left eye

we touch foreheads

i tell her

you aint ugly

get to my shoveling

i know why

folks call her

ugly or beast

or whatnot

i been called

lots of names too

some folks just dont

see things proper

sure she all wrinkled

an got a funny nose

an ears big enough

to make lookers laugh

but they missing somethin

so important

they not having

a good up-close

honest look

in her eye

all her beauty there

in her eye

it look like

a topaz marble

a boy once showed me

an her pretty eye

have long lashes

that flutter like

a little birds wing

a big beautiful

round eye

full of feelings

she cant speak

its all in there

the color of

sweet honey

or maybe

the color of

god hisself

sometimes i wonder

if that aint god

in there

when i look her

in the eye

so beautiful

only a dang

stupid person

would call

the Elephant

ugly

I know I'm going and I want to go. There is just this one significant worry which is staying me here in this painful life.

I've been dying for a while. A torturously long and slow while. I do believe I knew that death was imminent before I stepped foot on that bridge. For days now I have felt the swirling eddies of the dream-world coming to comfort me and to escort me to the other place. I so want to go there. Where I might at last be reunited with my loved ones. Which has been my one and only desire since I was put on that boat when I was just a little girl-calf. Before that even, when I was taken away from my mother before my proper weaning time.

But I am afraid to let go, and allow my spirit to spin off into the peaceful eddy. It is not that I am afraid to leave this place. I have never felt at home in this strange land. I am not even afraid to leave this mahout, William. I care deeply for him, as he has taken good care of me, but he does not need me. His life here also seems to be one not of his choosing, and perhaps he will find some semblance of freedom if he is relieved of my care. That is my wish for him.

No, my only hesitation is in regard to the dispensation of my bones. I have great fear, the greatest fear I have ever known actually, of what will happen to my bones when I depart from them and this Earth.

My kind, the Pachyderm, knows that our bones are the most sacred part. That they are the only part of us that remains. And that at the very center of the bones we remain. Little particles of the Pachyderm remain in the marrow. Forever. We have always known this. We have important rituals when one of us passes on. We gather around the dead in silence, and we touch the body, sharing our thoughts and hearing the spirits departing thoughts. We wait in mourning at the time of death and remember the loved one, observing as the body wilts and the spirit transcends. We wait for nature to make the bones clean and we bury our dead to preserve the bones forever in the final resting place which should be the same spot where the physical life ended. My kind can smell the presence of our bones and that is why I know I am the only one of my kind in this entire strange land. Because in all the thousands of miles I have been forced to walk across this place I have encountered no elephant bones at all. Not a trace of a scent of my kind, alive or dead, ever. So I must worry... What will become of my bones? My kind will not be able to find me here. I am sure of it. I do know humans bury their own in this land, but know not how or if I will be interred. They are flesh eaters and I fear I will be consumed. That they will gnaw my bones clean. And then what? None of the rest of me matters, I know that, but my bones are sacred, and I do not trust these people to care for my bones properly. Not even the mahout William. Perhaps he will see to my bones, but he has little say in matters. I doubt he will be free to do so even if he knows that he should. ... Oh my, oh my, what will become of the dead me in this barn? I should have been left at the river's edge. It was not right to drag me here. It is only right to let an elephant return to the Earth in the place where he last lay. I am in agony. My bones are broken, and there is no honor here in death. None.

So I have been fighting off the pull of the eddy, all the colors of the rainbow spiraling around and away and calling out to me. I am afraid to go, but soon I must relent. The pull is as strong as that of a great bull elephant. The pain is so severe it causes me to become unconscious in fits. It is then that I go to the place of remembering. Of when I was a baby in a memory of seventeen elephants. Remembering how the elders always circled around me, always protecting and caring for me, and teaching me the ways of us. Of my participation in my grandmother's funeral. Of the burial of her bones by my mother and her sisters. Of how I smelled and spoke to her in silence. Of how I threw straw upon her body too. Of returning to the site of her bones many months later, sensing its location with our trunks, where every elephant in the memory paused to communicate with the bones of our matriarch. Of it all making sense. Of it all being beautiful. And is it too much to ask this one thing of these strange people in this strange land? Just this one thing. Please... I implore you... make sacred my bones. -- Phir milenge.

Bore da dear sister,

I shall leave it
to your prudent judgement
which of your young should hear
this most distressing news.

She died this day.
September the 23rd.

The Elephant

is dead.

She suffered a fall
off a high bridge
landing on rocks below.
A man killed, another injured.

The rest of us were spared.
I had to pull the negro off her
and take him out of the barn
when the next thing was done.

Never seen him so distraught.
He gave up his breakfast
into the trees, when the doctor
pulled out his knives and instruments.

Negroes are so childish.
The animal was already dead.
Wasn't like the operation
was going to hurt her none.

Something had to be done
with her remains,
the weight of which
was several tons.

How could I reduce the loss
this tragic turn of events
will cost me? The learned men
of this town helped me decide.

I hired the doctor to skin
the Elephant.
We will keep the head,
feet and tail intact.

I aim to have it all
stuffed and mounted
by an expert taxidermist.
It will be a fine thing.

A fine way to let the people
keep right on seeing
the Elephant
for many years forward.

The rest of her is to be buried
on the hill in this village.
Soon as I can get that negro
to dig a big enough hole.

He's grieving fiercely.
I'm feeling low too.
Feelings don't matter none
when there's work to be done.

We covered the head so he
don't have to look on it.
Have to pack it on ice and ride
to Boston as quick as we can.

I pray that you are all faring better,

that you got your harvest in safely,

and that you're all settling into life

in America with contentment.

I hold you and yours

in my heart always,

your brother,

W. Owen

it was the durn

saddest of times

it surely was

it grieves me

to speak of it

we was fixing to leave

the state of vermont

and cross over

into new hampshire

it was mornin

a nice fall day

pretty blue sky

soft breeze blowin

master an me

was on our horses

way to the back

monkey was with me

mos the time we lead

the Elephant

our own selves but in that town

of putney we was escorted out

major curtis was his name

an his man name of sampson

was riding with him

they was leading

i pretty sure

the major wanted

to feel important an

mister felt a debt

well she aint never cared

for crossing bridges

thats on account of

how smart she is

its the way you handle her

that gets her to go

an she trusts me I'm

the elephant

keeper

but dont nobody

give an elephant paddy

what I think

i knew better

we got to the bridge

gaja-girl she balked

from the git-go

even shook her head no

see she real smart

an hears real good

with them big ole ears

course she does

she heard the loud

rushing water far below

river was high from rains

an making a white foam

so rough i feeling a little

fear of it myself

its a bad sound

she wasnt having it

thats when they

shouldve let me

do the driving

but they took to whipping her

i passed the monkey

to master but he tole me

stay in the saddle

let them be

she gave her ears

some angry flaps

an started to walk

slow scared steps

all is well master said

but it werent

i cant tell the rest

heres the newspaper clipping

would you be so kind

as to read it to me

i aint never learned

how to read

The Keene Sentinel
September 23, 1803

BREAKING NEWS

It falls on our lot to record

a most disastrous event

which forcibly reminds us how

uncertain are our possessions,

and in the midst of life we are in death.

In our last, mention was made

of the recent arrival of

The Elephant.

On their way to Westmoreland,

they attempted to pass

over the Connecticut River.

The owner and a colored man,

were on horses to the rear of

The Elephant.

They passed in safety

until near the gate on this side.

In consequence

of some delay in opening it,

The Elephant

slipped between the last pier

and the abutment.

The men in front advanced

and were in the act of spurring

The Elephant

forward with their whips,

when one of the cross timbers

on that side of the bridge

suddenly gave way, and

The Elephant,

the two riders and their horses

were precipitated together

with the falling timbers and planks

a distance of forty-six feet

on to the rocks!

The two horses

were instantly killed.

Major Curtis, his thigh broken,

his head much bruised

received such injury in the spine

that he lived but four hours

retaining his senses to the last.

The colored man

had a broken leg only

which was amputated

and is likely to do well,

but

The Elephant

weighing between 3 and 4 tons,

the reader would naturally suppose

was instantly killed.

Not so.

He appears to have fallen

on his back of breach,

and is doubtless injured internally,

but it is difficult to ascertain

to what extent.

Wednesday morning he was raised

upon his feet by shackles,

but was unable to bear his weight,

and appears to have little use

of his hind legs.

In the afternoon,

they got him upon an ox-sled,

and with eight yoke of oxen,

assisted by men with drag ropes

drew him up the steep bank

and took him to

a barn on the hill

in the village

where the noble animal lies

in much distress.

William
Amherst, Massachusetts
November, 1803

thats pretty much the truth

i could scarcely

believe mine own eyes

worse than what i seen

was what i heard

a god-awful sound

i could hear

the screams of gaja

an the two men

coming back to us

from the depths below

pitiful cries

same time master turned

his horse around

an yelled for me to come

he rushed back to get help

but i disobeyed

an climbed down

an across the rocks

even forgot that i cant swim

i was sorry to see

sampson suffer so

i was not sorry to see

the major close to dead

men tended to the men

i tended to gaja i am

the elephant

keeper

she was hurt bad

i tole em all

she couldnt get up

gave her what comforts i could

i was so sorry

for what happened

but what I mos felt

was angry

i couldnt barely

stand for it

when they drug her

up the hill like that

finally got her

in the barn

mister said hes

going to charge

people a nickel

for to see

the dying elephant

an he did

most of the folks

was kind and worried

they brung her treats

it was a comfort

i tried to understand

what gaja was trying

to say to me

she'd no reason to be sorry

i figure i know

because me and gaja

we lived likewise lives

i think she knew it

mister owen

he worried too

worried that his money maker

was going to die

i kep looking

for a chance

to steal his gun

to end her suffering

after a week of it

mercy took her

to the other side

i was mighty thankful

heres the other

newspaper clipping

careful you dont

tear it please

An elephant was forced by piking
to cross the river
on the Westmoreland Bridge.
He had nearly reached the end
upon the east side
when a portion of the bridge
being somewhat decayed
gave way, and the poor beast
fell with a despairing wail
about the crash of timbers
but he caught his trunk
around some of the under-braces,
and there in mid-air
he held on, all the time uttering
the most piercing shrieks of fright,
but this was of short duration.
He could not long support
his ponderous weight, and
he fell to the rocks beneath,
his back broken,
life remained for a few days.
The Elephant's skin was stuffed,
to be sent to the Boston Museum.

Will, I've made some decisions

about what will transpire henceforth,

for me, for you, and for the monkey.

I assure you I did the best I could

by all of us.

You've been a good and dutiful servant

and it is my truest desire

to do as well by you

as circumstances will allow.

Last night, at meeting with Mr. Savage,

it was agreed that

the Elephant,

that is that her body,

will be exhibited in a nice museum.

The papers say it offers "a vast deal

of rational amusement for very little money"

so people can continue to enjoy her

long into the future.

I should think that would please you.

I know you weren't pleased

about the skinning and stuffing,

but it's a fine place for her.

Mr. Savage is a famous artist.

There's a painting in the museum

he did of General George Washington.

Something else should please you –

the Elephant

is going to be set up along with

two living turtles that come from

the Island of Ascension

that you spoke of stopping by

when you brought her to America.

In any event,

I intend to return to my home in New York

and resume farming and droving.

So ... while I'm not happier for it

from this day forward

you belong to a man named

Hachaliah Bailey.

You, your horse, and the monkey.

Now, listen,

here's the part you'll like;

as the great overseer would have it,

Will, we've all been provided for.

Mister Savage, of this city,

has brought to America

the second elephant!

She's here now!

Sailed from London on that big ship

anchored in the harbor.

He's selling her to Bailey

to take her on tour.

You'll be her keeper!

Look over yonder,

see her coming.

This one's from Africa, Will.

Your own home land!

i couldnt

make no words

come out my mouth

i walk to her

slowly

put out my hand

i reach my arms

round her head

commenced to sobbing

the white men walk off

went inside the fancy house

had dinner by candlelight

BIG BETTE
IN A BARN AT BOSTON, MASSACHUSETTS
JANUARY 1804

I CAN SAY THAT I AM INDEED THANKFUL TO BE BACK UPON TERRA FIRMA. OH YEBO, OH YES. PRAISES FOR THE SOLID EARTH. THE WARM SOIL. THE GREEN TREES. BUT I WANT TO MOVE STILL FURTHER ON. TO REJOIN MY KIND, WHERE EVER THEY MAY BE. BUT THAT IS ABOUT THE EXTENT OF WHAT I AM THANKFUL FOR. WELL, ALSO FRESH VEGETATION, THOUGH THESE SPECIMENS ARE LESS THAN TASTY, THEY ARE FAR SUPERIOR TO THE CRUD I WAS BEING FED ABOARD THAT GOD FORSAKEN SHIP. OTHERWISE, I AM SORRY TO SAY, I AM LESS THAN HAPPY, AND THAT, YOU MAY NOT BE AWARE, IS A MOST UNNATURAL STATE FOR AN ELEPHANT. I HAVE BECOME ILL WITH A MELANCHOLY THAT PRESSES UPON ME FROM ABOVE LIKE A HEAVY BLACK RAINCLOUD. I HAVE BEEN WAITING FOR A THUNDER CLAP OR A LIGHTNING BOLT, TO FINALLY COME FROM WITHIN IT, AND JUST TAKE MY LIFE. I HAVE CARED LITTLE FOR LIVING FOR A LONG TIME. SO LONG. WHEN I WAS A YOUNG CALF I DIDN'T OBJECT STRENUOUSLY TO BECOMING DOMESTICATED, EVEN THOUGH IT WAS BY FORCE. THERE WAS SOME NOBILITY IN IT, AT THE BEGINNING. BEING OF SERVICE TO OTHERS, ESPECIALLY THOSE WHO ARE NOT AS CAPABLE AS YOU, IS NOBLE. I WAS NOT OPPOSED TO THE ARRANGEMENT WHEN THERE WAS SOME DEGREE OF FAIRNESS IN THE EXCHANGE, AND THAT EXCHANGE ITSELF WAS MARKED BY KIND INTERACTIONS. BUT THAT WAS LONG AGO AND I HAVE BEEN MOVED SO MANY TIMES AND HAVE SEEN SO MANY PLACES WHERE I AM NOT COMFORTABLE AND BEEN SUBJECTED TO SO MANY HANDLERS. SOME OF THEM I BECAME QUITE ATTACHED TO AND YET THEY LEFT ME ANYWAY. MOST WERE NOT WORTHY OF ATTACHMENT HAVING HARDLY MORE INTELLECT THAN A COMMON TREE MONKEY DRUNK ON MARULA FRUIT. NOW I HAVE BEEN DELIVERED NOT BACK TO MY HOME LAND AS I TRUSTED WAS TO BE MY REWARD. BUT TO THIS PLACE. ANOTHER STINKING CITY FULL OF HUMANS AND THEIR REFUSE, AND I HAVE NEVER BEEN SO COLD. THE COLD ENTERS MY FEET FROM BELOW AND TRAVELS UP MY LEGS. I MUST FLAP MY

EARS TO KEEP THEM FROM FREEZING. THE DESIGN OF THESE EARS WAS MEANT TO KEEP ME COOL.

I CAN TELL THIS IS NOT MY HOMELAND. I DIDN'T THINK THAT I COULD BEAR IT WHEN I DETERMINED THAT FACT SHORTLY AFTER OUR ARRIVAL. I REALLY DID NOT. WHEN I WAS DELIVERED TO MORE STRANGERS AND MY LEG WAS CHAINED IN THIS NEW BARN I CALCULATED HOW I COULD TEAR DOWN THE WALL WITH MY LEG IF I USED ALL OF MY STRENGTH, AND PICK UP ANY OF THE MEN THAT CAME NEAR ME. SIMPLY PICK THEM UP AND CRACK THEM AGAINST A BEAM IN THEIR OWN FILTHY BUILDING. THE ONE THAT CAGES ME HERE. I COULD DESTROY EVERYTHING IN SIGHT UNTIL FINALLY ONE OF THEM WOULD HAVE THE GOOD SENSE AND THE SKILL TO END MY LIFE WITH ONE OF THEIR WEAPONS, USUALLY FAIRLY CLOSE AT HAND. MY SADNESS HAD COALESCED AT JUST THAT TIME INTO A VOLUPTUOUS RAGE, AND I WANTED TO USE ALL OF MY PENT UP ENERGY, STORED IN ME ALL OF THOSE MONTHS IN THE BOAT'S BELLY, AND WAS ABOUT TO LET LOOSE IN A RAMPAGE OF FURY, THAT WOULD END IT ALL, END THEM ALL. THEN I WAS UNCHAINED AND ABOUT TO BE WALKED, TO STRETCH MY LEGS, AND I DECIDED, PERHAPS I WOULD BE MORE SUCCESSFUL OUTSIDE ON THE COBBLE STONED STREET. I COULD RUN, A PLEASURE DENIED OF ME FOR SO LONG, STAMPEDE AND KNOCK DOWN HUMANS AND FRIGHTEN HORSES AND EXACT MORE REVENGE AND ATTENTION TO MY CAUSE. ALL CREATURES WOULD SCRAMBLE OUT OF MY WAY AS IT WOULD BE OUT ON THE GREAT SAVANNAH. AS IT SHOULD BE. SO I ALLOWED MYSELF TO BE REMOVED FROM THE BARN.

AND THAT IS WHEN I MADE THE ACQUAINTANCE OF THE NEW MAHOUT. I BELIEVE HIM TO BE FROM MY HOME LAND. HE DOESN'T SEEM TO BELONG HERE EITHER. HE SHOWED ME THAT THE MEASURE AND THE CONTENT OF HIS HEART IS THE SAME AS MY OWN. SO YEBO, I DECIDED TO SPARE THESE PEOPLE. FOR NOW. I AM GOING TO TRUST THAT THIS NEW KEEPER SLEEPING IN THE HAY WITH ME JUST NOW, WILL GOOD GOD-OF-ALL WILLING, WALK US TO THE WIDE OPEN PLACE WHERE WE BELONG, WHERE WE WILL FIND OUR LONG LOST KIN, AND WHERE WE MAY BE FREE.

Excuse the intrusion.

I know you've work to do

but I'd like for my children,

Nathaniel and Elouisa,

to have a look at

the Elephant.

I recognize you,

though you've grown tall.

You were but a boy

when we were together aboard

the *America*.

My name is Hathorne.

I'm a captain now.

I'm gratified to see

that you're still tending

the Elephant.

I knew Captain Crowninshield

had sold her, but,

what is your name,

but William, I'm now thinking

that this isn't the same elephant?

I thought as much!

I remember her features

were different. She was smaller.

How she would spray me

with her trunk!

Son, this is the second elephant

to come to our country.

Look at the ears. She's from Africa.

We shall find that place

on our map at home.

William, my good man,

please take this ha'dollar

with my gratitude.

Be well and take good care of

the Elephant.

Drover Hachaliah Bailey
a tavern at Boston, Massachusetts
Summer 1805

It just goes to show
how events can work out
as you wish, if
you work hard enough
and have faith.

I remember so well
back in ninety-six
at the Bull's Head Tavern.
I so wanted to buy
the first elephant in America.

But she went for the monstrously
large sum of ten thousand dollars!
An elephantine sum.
I was there. I saw
the Elephant.

Never stopped thinking about it
all these years thence.
Read of the second one
arriving at Boston.
Knew an animal from a warm clime
couldn't be kept there.

I saw my chance.
Mister Savage, a smart man,
agreed to my offer of $1000.
and I became the owner of
the Elephant.

The public is not likely to know
that this is a different elephant

and we will allow that belief
to perpetuate - for now.
Her keeper, her monkey, and I.

Owen never named his elephant.
He had the newspapers call her
The Elephant.
But I have already named
this big girl.

For another most adored
girl of mine;
My daughter Elizabeth Anne Bailey,
My little Bette.
This here is Big Bette.

yeah

i thought things

would be pretty much

the same as before

i s'pose

it looks that way

to mos folks

master, negro, elephant

walking all over creation

same as before

but that aint the truth

been lots of changes

somes good some aint

new master bailey

got lots of new

high-falutin ideas

each one sound

like a lot more work

for me

some men got to learn

the hard way

stead of listening

i was fierce fond

of the first elephant

my gaja-girl i called her

this new elephant

is a good girl too

jus different is all

gaja was a baby

when they brought her

i raised her up

this one come fully growed

much more wrinkled

african not indian

got much bigger ears

some female tusks

theys jus big teeth is all

much is the same

about her as gaja

we get along right fine

an elephant is an elephant

a man is a man

jus some little differences

little differences

that shouldn't make no matter

at all

Of course I need to make some changes.
This is my livelihood.
I need the keeper to understand that.
I want him to teach
the Elephant
some more amusing tricks.

I intend to purchase more animals
we can pull along in cages.
And we must take to traveling by night.
Far too many people
are getting a free look at
the Elephant.

*William
on the road
1806*

now he's wanting to choose

what sorts of tricks

the Elephant

an i will do

he dont pay no mind

to the proper order

of my teaching her things

when we do a show

he starting to do

all the talkin and hollerin

wants me to do tricks

at his orders

like i'm an animal too

biggest problem is

me and bette we

pretty tired mos the time

i'm trying to get him

to understand that walkin

by day is better

its walking that keeps

the Elephant

happy - its to her liking

keeps her in good spirits

keeps her in good health

these are important considerations

she always lifting her snout

sniffing for something

she cant never seem to find

she know when she need to stop

she can smell water

from way far off

makes a elephant real content

to take a good soak

an get all clean

then come out

an get all

dirty again

she even pick

some stalks and

clean her own ears

i been telling him

its important she be happy

or she become ornery

i been telling him

it cost less money

to let her eat what she find

she eat tree bark

all sorts of stuff

she find by day

a sick elephant

aint no good

to nobody

but dont you worry none

we gonna be rich

thats what he says

Seamstress Ona Judge Staines
Portsmouth, New Hampshire
June 1806

I knew it was a bold

and cockamamie plan

as soon as I conceived of it.

My children needed

a pleasant diversion

morseso even then I,

and they deserved one.

So we went on the long walk

to get to the barn where I knew

the Elephant

to be staying. I timed it so we'd arrive

after all of the townfolk, the white folk,

had already been entertained.

It was a warm June evening.

Light lingering late.

I could hear insects, frogs croaking,

but little else. I hushed the children

led them along the edge of the property,

where we waited and watched.

Then I heard it, from inside the barn,

a man singing, a black man's voice.

I felt less afraid at the sound.

I called upon my boldness again,

got out my three coins,

slid the barn door open.

Good evening, sir.

I'm sorry to intrude,

but I seek your indulgence

for the sake of my children.

I have thirty cents

so that they might see

your circus animals.

He stared in silence, then,

"Yes'm, please, come closer

and meet Big Bette."

I introduced us.

He doffed his cap.

"Not often I get called sir.

I'm William, the elephant keeper."

My little Liza asked him

to sing the song again.

He tickled

the Elephant

under the chin, leaned close to her eye,

nudged her right toes with his

and began to sing:

My mammy gimmee fifteen cents

for to see the elephant jump the fence.

He jump so high, I didn't see why,

if she gimme a dollar he might not cry.

So I axed my mammy

to gimme a dollar,

For to go an hear

the elephant holler

he holler so loud,

he scared the crowd!

Next he jumped so high,

He reach the sky,

An he won't get back

'fore the fourth of July!

I couldn't remember when

my children had such lighthearted fun.

Their smiles were such a gift.

Something I could hold in my heart

and pull out when need be.

I offered him our coins.

"No ma'am, use that for something

the children might need."

I had the children thank him and

the Elephant

while the monkey scolded.

It felt hard to leave the barn.

As we slipped out

Will the elephant keeper

looked at me with a

face so full of sadness.

Our looks conveyed so much

that would never, could never

be spoken.

i was having regrets

bout coming so far north

travel was rough

folks not getting along

big barns and spare coins

was getting scarce

but one day there

something happened

a tribe of indians

come walking into town

come walking slow and sad

like theys going to a funeral

then i see they was nervous

bout if theyd be welcome

i know that kind of worry

i waved em close

one look like the grandpap

stepped up

looked to a younger man

to speak

the younger one

said the family had no money

but they like to give me

this beautiful basket

made out a porkypine quills

if i let their daughter

a lil indian princess see

the Elephant

i couldnt say no

did one of our best tricks

the man say

this is sarah molasses

princess of the penobscot people

so i say

bette bow for the princess

and nudge her knee

she kneel down

present her trunk

all elegant like

i peeked a look

at the princess

she didnt smile

but her eyes shone happy

i think old bette

felt the same tug as me

she did her best

for that princess

they didnt clap or cheer

when we done

jus nodded they thanks

turned and walked away

quiet as they came

leaving some they sadness

behind

i was glad they could lay

some of it down

Well, I'll be the dang monkey's uncle,
Will, come here a minute,
I want to read you something.
Something I think will be
of a particular interest to you.
Now listen here;

The Congress of these United States
has recently passed an act to prohibit
the importation of slaves
into any port or place
from any foreign kingdom or country
any negro, mulatto, or person of color,
with intent to hold, sell, or dispose
of such as a slave ...

Ten thousand dollars is a mighty steep fine!
Twenty thousand for outfitting a slave ship!
Ho-lee cow! President Jefferson signed the law.
Next thing you know they'll be outlawing
the importation of elephants!
Dang. Pass me that jug.

Articles of Agreement

Between Hachaliah Bailey of the first part,

and Brunn and Lent of the second part.

Brunn and Lent agree to pay

the aforesaid Bailey twelve hundred dollars

for the equal two thirds

of the earnings of

the Elephant

for one year from the first day of the month.

Bailey on his part furnishes one third

of the expenses and Brunn and Lent

the other two thirds.

Those who wish to gratify their curiosity

by seeing the wonderful works of nature,

will do well to call.

Perhaps the next generation

may never have the opportunity

of seeing an elephant again,

as this is the only one in the United States,

and perhaps the last visit to this place.

sometimes i git tired too

i know i shouldnt complain

know theys no reason

to bother complaining

know theys lots of worse

lives i could be livin

i have lived some of em

i have seen plenty of em

with my own eyes

i seen men beaten and broken

til not much left of em

i seen families in chains

sold apart at the market

but every time i git settled

into a way of doing things

or meet some nice folks

i got to move on

107

now he says i'm to have

this white man with a lion

travel along with us

another one stolen from africa

to make for a better show

to make more money

thats what he wants

the lion makes

the Elephant

skittish cause she smart

makes me skittish too

someone should care

how

the Elephant

feels

maybe if the lion

eats the monkey

someone will pay heed

The day
the Elephant
arrived
I heard them coming quick enough
that I was outside to watch them walk up the road.
Went out to be welcoming, not to get
a free look which seemed to be the owner's concern.
Stood out near my forsythia bushes waiting.
The owner greeted me, and I, him.
I invited the party to fill themselves at our well.
As they did, I decided to offer lodging to all.

I've a large barn that hasn't been home
to any animals since my husband's passing.
I'm not a tavern, and my sister and I don't
care for drinking on our property,
but we have for many years
kept a comfortable tramp room there
that's likely to meet all a man's needs.

It was great fun for Dottie and I
to have an elephant as a guest.
Had both our iron spiders sizzling.
Fried chicken, oysters, salt pork beans.
Sent cousin Clyde to fetch a jar of my
dilly pickled green beans.
When next I saw Mister Bailey

pass by the back door
I issued an invitation
right through the window.

He came to dinner, but he came alone,
leaving the rest of his party in the barn.
Well, I don't much care for
letting my cooking turn cold,
so I excused myself rather quickly
saying I needed to tend to something
in the kitchen, which wasn't untrue.
I spooned a scoop of everything
on a big china plate,
covered it with a napkin,
filled a jar with cold sweet tea,
headed out back.
No one that stays on my farm goes hungry.
Not while I'm alive.

i heard her working the big barn door

with her little miss foot

i slid it open

there was the lady of the house

she held out a plate

and jar of tea

to me

the elephant keeper

put the pitch fork down

wiped my hands on my trousers

not sure where to look

stared at the plate easy enough

oh i thank you maam

that is right kind of you

then i tole her

i knew when I saw

that kitty-cat

painted on you fence post

that a kind person

live here

He seemed a trustworthy sort.
It was perfectly clear
the Elephant
thought so,
and the rude little monkey too.
I passed him the plate,
pulling off the napkin.
His eyes went wide which I guess
was the glad reaction
I was looking for.
I pointed to my old milking stool.
Please don't let it get any colder.
Took a few minutes to visit with
the Elephant
who really is a friendly girl
while he ate with a good gusto.

Mind if I ask you a question?
He wiped his mouth and nodded.
*If you could live a life of your own choosing
what would you do?*
He took a draw of tea, then,
*I really do like working with animals
and I'm good at it.
I'd like to have a little farm,
a little place of my own.*

He paused, looked away,
I'd like to have a wife
and family of my own.

After a bit he added
mind if I axe you a question?
Ma'am, why you so nice?
I didn't know what to say
and so said nothing.
Ma'am, in all my years of travel
cross all of these states
I can count on my hands
the times anybody
treated me this kindly
so I's just wondering
what it is makes you so?
A shrug, a smile.
I bid him good night
taking the lantern
leaving them
in the almost dark
of a warm night.

A night brimful
of bright stars
and old questions.

The brothers Josey and Danny Nelson
Newington, New Hampshire
August 1810

(a poem in three voices)

Finish your blasted chores Danny.
We got to see
the Elephant!

Get that wood box filled quick!
I done everything in the barn
with not one lick of help from you!

                    Well you keep cuffing me
                    in the head
                    ain't making me go faster!

Finish, and get it done right.
I got to go swipe some coins
out of Grandma's secret can.

                    Why don't we just ask her?
                    I think she give us two quarters to see
                    the Elephant.
                    We been good –
                    some of the time.

Nah, I'm just gonna take 'em.
It's easier than 'splaining everything.
Got to yell every word at her.

And what if she want to come?
Take her half a day to walk there.
Just shut up and don't say nothing.

***

Come on, Danny!
I got 'em.
Let's go!

***

Yeah, I mean yes sir,
we got the quarters.
We got to be up front,
please.

Wow, Josey,
You see that trick?
He obey real good, don't he?

Yep, zounds,
that was really good!

What's he gonna do now Josey?
What's he gonna do?

Shut up and listen!

Ladies and gentlemen! Boys and girls! For your own safety please step back, as **the Elephant** keeper will now hand over his whip to the giant beast to do with as he pleases! … That's it, that's it, step back! … **The Elephant** is not at all afraid of that whip, as you saw for yourself. A nick of that whip, which would hurt you fiercely, has no effect on the great quadruped at all. How could it? His hide is so thick and tough that it is bullet proof! Now watch as the keeper has **the Elephant** crack the whip and make a ring all around his great self! He will be turning all the way around in a circle made wide by the whip he is holding. Mind your children, and yourselves.

Bravo!

Bravo!

Look at him bow down!

More please!

One more trick please! More!

More!

***

What you cuff me in the head for!?

Cuz you don't need to kick

every rock in the road

all the way home.

You hear what that man said about that
elephant, Josey?

Course I did.

I heard every word he said.

What you talking about?

Talking 'bout he said

that elephant's hide

so thick its bullet proof.

What that mean?

Don't be such a blasted dope Danny,

bullet proof mean

there ain't no bullet

can penetrate through

the skin and hurt

the Elephant.

That's what I thought it meant.

-- That true Josey?

Not sure. Not sure how the man can say such a thing

'less he tried it. So maybe he tried it and he know.

But maybe he's just lying. Sure enough, there weren't

no bullet holes in the Elephant's skin.

I looked him over pretty good.

Maybe we should try it Josey?

I sure like to see some bullets

bounce off that old elephant.

That'd be a great story

we'd have to tell the other boys.

Yeah it sure would!

Maybe you finally

had a good idea Danny.

***

Git down, you fool!

I tole you to stay in the cover of the berry bushes.

We'll hear 'em easy enough when they set out.

I'mma cleanup Grandpa's ol long rifle again.

Want these bullets to shoot real nice and smooth.

I want to do the shooting, Josey.

It aint fair you git to shoot. It was my idea!

I got the gun, not you, may be too much for you to handle.

Anyway, that's one big animal, moves real slow.

Might be enough time for us both to take a shot.

I been thinking that the best way to get a bullet in

the Elephant would be to aim for a tender place.

What place that be Josey?

We should aim for its eye.

Bet the bullet would go in the eye.

Eyes is always soft.

I dun know Josey. Won't that hurt

the Elephant?

You such a dat burn baby Danny.

***

They coming! They coming!

Lay low. I'm going behind that tree.

***

(..................ready ... aim ... fire!)

BANG, BANG, BANG!

I hit her! I hit her! Run, they coming after us.

Run home, Danny, run!

      I hear her honking Josey. She sound mad.

***

      I hear you crying in that pillow.

      Why you still crying, Josey?

Cuz my dat burn bum hurts so much.

All on account of your stupid idea.

      How many times Grandpa switched you?

I dun no. Lost count.

Said we had to see how tough my hide was.

Switched me til his arm got tired.

Said tomorrow you'd get yours.

'Scuse me sir.

May I speak with you a moment?

It is quite important.

Don't want no free look.

It's something else I have to say,

If you don't mind, sir.

I'd like to join your little circus.

I'm a smart boy, already schooled,

and I've a long history with your elephant.

I have read about elephants

in the encyclopedia,

so may I please join up with you?

Mister Hachaliah Bailey

That so!?
Here that Will?
Boy's got a history with Bette.

He must be smart,
if he's read about elephants
in the dat burn encyclopedia.

Nearly grown you say.
Come now boy,
how old are you?

And what is
this history
that you speak of?

Nathaniel Hathorne Junior

I'm nearly ten.
My father, whom I'm named for,
sailed the first elephant to America
with that blackie
back before I was born.

Then he took me to meet them
when you came to Massachusetts.
I was just a little boy then,
but I'm now ready to make
my way in the world.

I am sure I should be
your next elephant keeper
but for now I could maybe
help with that monkey
and do other chores for you.

My father, the captain, he died
of the yellow fever
after he left Surinam,
a place real far away.
Mother brings us here each summer.

She's got my sisters to take care of,

and my uncle to take care of her,

and I have one dollar and a half

and my bag here all packed.

I am ready to go.

Mister Hachaliah Bailey

Tell you what
you're going to do boy.
You're going to git
your sorry little hind side
back home
twice as fast as you got it here,
and if you're lucky, I won't
take a switch to you as you go.

You're going to git home
and git into your bed,
and give thanks that you got one,
nice warm one I bet it is too.
And you won't ever
give your mother another
reason to cry or worry
what's become of you!
You hear what I'm saying?

Hold up, boy,
just one thing
before you go.
How about we let
this ole elephant
give you a ride home?

Well, baby Bette,
here's something
you'll be happy to know.

Papa had been away so long
I was afraid I'd forget him.
I wanted to run off and join him
on his tour of the states.

I knew I could be
of much help to him.
Tried talking to Mama
about it many a time.

I know she also disfavors
Papa being away so many months
for I've heard her say as much
many a time.

She doesn't seem to welcome
his return at planting time
for she is usually left
with another baby on the way.

She has never really approved
of what she calls
his elephant scheme.

Mama thinks she's likely to die
of working this farm and
raising us children alone.

She said Papa has a way
of wearing a wife right out,
she being his third.
I remind her that Papa said
we will soon sell this farm
for a mansion with a hundred rooms.

And a huge barn for all of the
exotic animals he'll acquire.

Mama will have many servants
to tend to us all.

Well, for quite some time
It'd been hurting my feelings
that Papa named
the first ever elephant in America
after you!

I tried not to let it gnaw at me
but some things just do.
I was his first born daughter.
I didn't see why he done that
for his second born daughter,
you not even old enough
to know such a fine thing
been done for you.
I was mad at you, baby Bette,
sorry about that.

Well, when Papa came home
I had no aim to bother him
with my melancholy
but to my surprise,
while we were in the barn visiting
the Elephant
he just noticed it for his own self
and asked me of it.
I had to tell him, to be obedient,
I blurted it out,
why'd you name Big Bette
after little Bette?
He laughed, and Hachaliah Bailey
is not a man that laughs often.
He set me down on a hay bale,
Like I were light as a hen feather,
and he talked to me, of his thoughts,
which is not something
Hachaliah Bailey does often.

I watched his beard bob up and down
like I used to do when I was your size.

He said not to fret, that he done it
with a plan in mind. Hachaliah Bailey
is a man of grand plans.
He said Big Bette was a name
that suited a great big quadruped,
and that both Bettes come to him
in the same year. He says
some year soon you'll ride upon
the Elephant

as part of the show, which would be charming

for the people to see, but Bette, Papa said

he was saving my name

for an animal not yet acquired,

but part of the grand plan.

Papa said one of the big cats,

beautiful and brave like me,

will share my name ~ Calista.

I hugged him for that, and you know

Hachaliah Bailey isn't a man

who tends toward hugging.

So it is no longer any worry to me

that you, little Bette,

have an ugly old elephant named for you.

I can be happy for you now.

Keep your smelly old elly.

I'm getting a lion

or maybe even a leopard.

evening

what state we in

oh yes maine

weve run into

jus every kind of folks on these roads

but never a muster of men like this

sign of the times

worried when i see yall comin

over the bend bearing arms

thought you might be

highway robbers

but here you are

all good men

going to portsmouth, going to defend

these united states

sure you can touch her

jus be slow and gentle

best you hold out your hand

she will shake if she trusts you

she wants a drink o your bottle

mind any papers your carrying

no no best not climb up on her

she bout ready to rest now

we'll go yonder out your way

but first

can I ask ya   there going to be

any black soldiers in your regiment

no she dont dance

no i dont dance

im an elephant keeper

come on bette

lets go girl

My dearest family,

With warmest regards
I write to inform you
of a change of plans.
We find our tour
to be much disrupted by war.
We continue to encounter men
leaving their homes defenseless
in defense of the nation.
At present, my intention
is to bring Big Bette home.
Please do begin working
on a large blanket for her
to winter over in the barn.
I am

with fond affection
your loving husband and father,

H. Bailey

Oh Mother!
Thank you for the birthday cake
and the new shirt.

But now that I've turned twelve
we need to speak of matters
of greater consequence.

Really, it is Father and I
that should have this discussion
as these are the matters of men.

Before too much longer
I'll be growing a beard like Papa
and will have the voice of a man.

There is a war on.
Every able-bodied man
must do his part.

As women and children
you can't hear the battle cry

but I sure do.

I shall be a soldier
and when I get back from battle
I'll assist Papa in the business.

The menagerie is growing
and Papa gets older every day.
My brothers can do the farm chores.

Why do you say be quiet and eat my cake?
That's not the way a woman
should speak to a man.

Yes, ma'am.
Sorry, ma'am.

Dear cousin Susan,

I received your letter
and rushed through my chores
before darkness comes
to write this prompt reply
of which you are so deserving.
We are all well.
Papa's hip ague doesn't
slow him down in the least.
He owns a sloop now,
for moving animals upriver.
He also owns a share
in the stage coach company here.
Most exciting of all,
he has acquired a bear.
A cage has been built
upon a wagon for her.
She'll be pulled along
perhaps by Big Bette.
Won't that be charming?

She is black and fat and
many a time, ferocious.
Papa has tasked the keeper
with keeping her calm.
Remember Little Lord Mondy?
He has a mate now.
Thy fight and love each other
in fits and starts.
One can conclude
spring is the time
for such romantic endeavors.
Even the elephant keeper
has found companionship
with mother's maid.
I believe they're courting.
Odd to see them smile so.
I think it nice to see
loneliness abated
in any of God's creatures,
and it makes me wonder
who will be my suitor?
Susan, do you suffer
such silly questions?
Mama is well, though tired.
She had a short confinement

with the birth of baby Steven.
For a total of seven children
in case you lost count.
Papa praised my assistance
and said I am exceptional
for a girl of fourteen years.
Too, he agrees with yours,
that the end of war
is close at hand.
Reinforcements have arrived
at nearby Niagara Falls.
But I fear my father
will then leave again.
Mother sends her love
to you and yours.
She also asks
if the sickness
has left your town, and
how many lives it took?

Kind regards,
your cousin,
Calista B.

Lewis Bailey
Baltimore, Maryland
August 1814

Dear Mother and children,

Papa said to write and tell you
that we are safe from harm,
lodged in the barn
of a fine Baltimore family.
It falls on me to tell you
of exciting events that unfolded.
You are likely unaware that you've
a great hero in the family.

Namely Old Bette, the hero elephant.
Perhaps you know of the attack
by British troops upon the Federal City,
with acts of great hostility.
Our people were fleeing in great numbers.
I, along with Will and the animals,
were sheltered in a barn.
We could hear the far off
noise of an attack by sea.
Papa and our landlord

climbed upon the roof
to surmise the situation.
Washington City was on fire!

Homes would burn. People perish.
When at last quiet came
Papa said we would move on.
In all honesty I must say
I've never seen nor imagined
such destruction as we found.
We rode along in silence.
Even the monkeys were still.

Along ravaged Pennsylvania avenue
Bette, with her great strength
cleared the road of much debris
blocking some from escape.
Hot and sooty beams she tossed
aside like autumn twigs.
We proceeded to the White House,
badly burned,
abandoned, aflame.

Will had Bette take water at the pump
and put out several fires.

She approached the heat
at his command
though all animals fear fire. Then,
as if providence sought vengeance,
a great storm rained upon the city
which kicked up a funnel cloud
that bore down the avenue.

Two flying canons came down upon
the bodies of a few unfortunate folks.
Bette lifted the great guns
off the crying survivors.
Between the brute power of the storm
and, I daresay, our elephant,
the British retreated!
O heroic Bette!

Mother, I know you feared
harm would come to me
on this journey. I assure you,
though great horrors occurred
I am unscathed by all of it
and have become a man
by way of witness.
Sincerely,
Lewis

We weren't sure if we should allow them to pass through,
never mind stop over for a show, but our children too,
even most of our full grown folks, wanted to see
the Elephant.

The owner of the menagerie claimed nothing like that
had happened before any place they'd ever been.
Seemed sincere so we gave him ten minutes
to subdue the beast before we put it down.
They understood and beat it within inches of its life
to save it.

The Elephant
is a wild animal, from the wilds of Africa.
Owner said it had never stampeded before
but I could see it was doing something
that comes quite natural.

They'd walked into Deep River, middle of the day,
strolled up the street, calm and easy.
Gave us no cause for concern, at first.
Then

about the time the wagons were coming up from the wharf
to unload a delivery of ivory just arrived
the Elephant
started trumpeting angry noises,
waving his big old trunk around.

Picked up a horse yoke, threw it up high,
smashed it to smithereens.
That's when we got our rifles out,
gave the owner a warning.

The Elephant
stampeded the public garden on our green.
Knocked his keeper on his keester.
Snapped the picket fence like kindling.
Attacked the flower beds, made a terrible
mess of the pretty ivory dust fertilizer
the gardeners will have to spread again.

I yelled for them to get out,
come back without animals to pay up,
or I'd sue, so yes, we did see
the Elephant.

boss bailey jus said

for me to do one more show

i knew thats what i d be doin

same as every day

he didnt need to tell me

what he really meant was

he was going to the tavern

i'll bring you some supper

be sure to get a coin from everyone

like i was likely to forget

first thing i seen was

a beautiful pair of draft horses

them horses was so big

even bette took notice

then i seen the wagon

handsome built buck board

jus chock full of people

they come along slowly

soon i could see

mos those people was chilren

the wagon pull up by

two men who look jus the same

had some funny haircuts

in the back was two ole ladies

clutching baskets close

too many chilren to count

every age cept sucklings

big ones holding little ones

some young ladies

donning clean white caps

looking so pretty i knew

to look away to be sure

not to cause no ruckus but

i couldnt look away fast enough

what my eyes got caught up on

was one of them young ladies

was negro

only she was sitting with the rest

right among em all

dressed zactly the same

i've traveled all over creation

an aint never seen that

she look jus like me but

only i seem to see it

i couldnt stop staring

an staring at any woman

can get a man like me

in a world of hurt

i tried to right myself

when one a the men jump down

i was trying to determine

how to save myself

when the man started talkin

calm like we's friends

that was peculiar too

said they brought the chilren to see

the Elephant

but first they need to know

if the animals was treated cruelly

you mean will they see the animals beat

no sir i'm fiercely fond of this elephant

i'd sooner take a beating than give her one

guess i said the right thing cause he said

those who are cruel to animals

are generally bad citizens

well the wagon full o folks

was all clean an tidy an quiet

as mouses as if they come up

on an elephant every day or so

one the men pull out his purse

i tell em all *welcome*

this here big bette she will hold

the pail out for you to drop

your coins in she'll come to you

then we did our trick

an she spects her reward

which is our last trick

that people always hoot about

she open a bottle of porter

and drink it all up

i got some hooting all right

the two ladies in the back

we don't want to see

the Elephant

drink spirits

so i invited the children

an the ladies

they could come on down

and feed her apples and see

the other animals

then the men waved me over

started talkin a blue streak

said they were shakers

something like the quakers

they got a big spread up in the hills

they call it the holy land

whole bunch of em live together

all holy like

mos them chilren aint they own

but they raising em up

well those men had some

genuine concern for me

we talked it out awhile

thats bout all im gonna say

bout that but

that was a right good day

and i hope to come back

to alfred maine some day

yessir

thats a good place i'd say

listen up bette

maybe you heard

some of that talk

with the merry dancers

maybe you didnt

imma tell you bout it

jus the same

mos the time its you

that gets a special invite

but back there

i got one

my own invitation

those people asked me

to come live with them

people called that

sound like they might be

fun to be roun

though i cant say

they looked like they was

merry or dancers

anyway i been thinkin on it

been chewin on it

like a stick in my teeth

all the way here

was even thinkin bout

if i should keep walkin

this direction

or step off in the woods

heres what i come to

my minds made up

i wont leave you

not while i got

a breath left in me

if we cant be free

together –

we'll be like this

– together

be hard enough

for those folks to

hide a negro man

jus no way for them

to hide an elephant

so you an me

jus keep on walkin

you keep sniffin

for what you lookin for

an i ll keep lookin

for something too

we might find it

i dont know

dont even know

what were lookin for

but i reckon we'll know it

when we find it

so thats that

lets get some rest

A word or look was sufficient

to stimulate him to the greatest exertions.

He caressed his master in the best manner,

and would not so readily obey another.

All his motions were majestic.

He kneeled on either side, raised his master

to his back with his trunk as directed,

or walked over the prostrate body

of the keeper at the proper bidding.

From the situation of his eyes,

he could not see his fore feet,

and calculated the distance to the object

over which he was to pass without injury:

so he carefully measured the space

before and after with his trunk,

then divided the distance so accurately

that the last step, before reaching the body,

was just near enough to afford him opportunity,

with a long stride, to accomplish his feat,

to the wonder of every beholder.

This was done with so much care and wisdom

that it would seem to proceed from a higher impulse

than that of a mere animal instinct.

He was a great traveler, kept pace

with the best horses of the company.

It was his custom in the autumn,

when passing orchards of tempting fruit

to remove two or three upper rails of the fence,

and stepping over, to make a meal of the apples,

then, without direction, to return to the road.

Little Bette Bailey
Bailey kitchen
January 1816

Mama! Mama!
Teacher gave me something
I don't understand why
or what it means, but
I think you'll want to hear it.
This was written by the editor
of the New York Times newspaper.

We have all our little troubles in this life,
and for those who are not too proud,
to use a popular phrase, it may be added,
that we have all our elephants to see.
It is narrated of a certain farmer
that his life's desire was to behold
this largest of quadrupeds,
until the yearning became
well nigh a mania.
He finally met one of the largest size
traveling in a menagerie.

159

His horse was frightened,

his wagon smashed,

his eggs and poultry ruined.

But he rose from the wreck radiant

and in triumph.

"A fig for the damage," quoth he,

"for I have seen

The Elephant!"

Isn't it a pretty story, Mama?

But what does it mean?

That must be our elephant.

Shall I read it again?

My dearest wife Mary,
and children; Calista,
Lewis, Little Bette,
Jane, Joseph, James,
and Steven,

I pray this finds you all safe and warm.
It has been weighing heavy upon my soul
to be so far away from you of late.
It grieves me something fierce.
I am sorry for it, and assure you all
that soon we will build a mansion
in one of the southern states
where the animals can live comfortably
and ourselves moreso.

I hope that this will be the last year
that you must endure such hardships
as you are now handling.
Lewis, keep an eye on how much snow
settles on the roofs of house and barn.
I know you will never forget
to tend to the wood pile.
All of you mind your mother.
We have reached the end
of our southern sojourn
and will now reverse our route
and make our way home.

I have heard some scuttlebutt
that there is another elephant
now on tour in America
so that is something to consider
as we continue to build
Bailey and Company's Splendid Menagerie.

I have purchased here in Georgia
a parcel of peanuts for you.
I fear the monkeys will steal them all
far in advance of our arrival.
You know how naughty Mondy is.

Also bought a sack of sweet potatoes.
Am sure they'll be mighty sweet
by the time we make it home to Somers.
Best regards from
your most affectionate father,

H. Bailey

Millwright David Daniels
grist mill at Shapleigh, Maine
April 1816

What in tarnation you talking about?
You can't put my mill up for auction!
Been in my family for forty-odd years.

You know dang well this is how
I make my living, such as it is!
I'm going to get along all right,

just takes a while to get things straight
after a man's brother and partner dies.
You ought to know that!

Things go up and down,
and come round right again.
The creditors have to wait, is all.

You see that wheel stone turning.
Not my fault we had a dang war!
Not my fault we've had so many frosts

not a farmer for miles got corn to grind
or got a dime to spend on meal!
You can't foreclose on me.

This mill business is in the public convenience.
What will folks do without a grist mill?
What you're fixing to do ain't Christian.

Get off my land and don't come back!
Take your lousy papers with you.
Writ of hogwash is what it is!

Big Bette
Just Outside Alfred, Maine
April 1816

YEBO, WILLIAM AND I WERE HAPPY. WE WERE LEAVING THE TOWN WILL LIKED SO MUCH AND HEADED SOUTH ON A WORN AND DUSTY ROUTE. IT WAS A NICE WALK. I WAS HEADED FOR A POND. I SMELLED WATER, AND KNEW THAT WE WOULD BE VEERING OFF THE ROAD AND HAVING A BATH. IT WAS OUR FAVORITE THING. MY OWNER HAD LONG AGO LEARNED NOT TO TRY AND PREVENT ME FROM GOING OFF THE ROAD FOR I'D ONLY DO IT WHEN MY NEEDS WERE LEGITIMATE AND NOT OTHERWISE BEING MET. HE'D CARRY ON AT THE SIDE OF THE ROAD FOR US TO HURRY AND RESUME THE MEETING OF HIS NEEDS. I'D PAY HIM NO HEED, THUS WILLIAM COULD'T PAY HIM ANY HEED EITHER. SO WE BOTH CHERISHED THOSE TIMES WHICH WERE NOT FREQUENT. WE'D PLAY AND BATHE AND SHOWER AND FROLIC. SOMETIMES WHEN I GOT OUT I'D ROLL AROUND ON THE GROUND TO GET MYSELF GOOD AND DIRTY, THEN DECIDE WHILE I'M DOWN THERE I MIGHT AS WELL TAKE A NAP. WILLIAM TOOK GREAT JOY IN THAT, WHEN HE GOT TO LIE DOWN BESIDE ME IN THE GRASS, WHILE THE BOSS HAD TO WAIT FOR US. AND I LIKE MAKING WILLIAM HAPPY.

AT THAT TIME, I HAD PICKED UP MY PACE IN ANTICIPATION OF OUR OUTING. THE POND WAS ONLY A FEW RODS AWAY. I SENSED A NAP IN OUR FUTURE. THAT IS WHEN I SMELLED THE MAN. WELL BEFORE I SAW HIM OF COURSE AND I NEVER SAW HIM AS CLEARLY AS I SMELLED HIM, BUT I DID SEE HIM, A FEW MINUTES LATER. HE WAS HIDING IN SOME SHRUBBERY ON THE LEFT SIDE OF THE ROAD, AND HOLDING A GUN. IT DIDN'T ALARM ME. IT WAS NOT A PARTICULARLY UNFAMILIAR SIGHT FOR ME, EXCEPT FOR THE FACT THAT THE MAN WAS NOT WEARING ANY CLOTHES. IT IS RARE FOR HUMANS TO VENTURE OUT WITHOUT CLOTHING, I HAVE ONLY SEEN IT DONE FOR

BATHING. I ASSUMED HE MIGHT HAVE JUST BEEN BATHING IN THE POND I WAS HEADED FOR. SO I NOTICED THAT ABOUT HIM, AND THAT HE REEKED OF ALCOHOL. I HAVE LITTLE INTEREST IN NAKED MEN IN BUSHES, BUT I HAVE DEVELOPED A FONDNESS FOR ALCOHOL. SEEING THAT HE POSSESSED ONLY A GUN AND NOT A BOTTLE, I WALKED ON WITHOUT ACKNOWLEDGING HIM. WILLIAM WAS WALKING AT MY RIGHT SHOULDER AS HE USUALLY DID WHEN NOT UPON A HORSE AND COULD NOT HAVE SEEN THE MAN.

I BELIEVE THAT I HEARD THE GUN BLAST BEFORE I FELT IT. THE SOUND WAS SO LOUD THAT IT ALONE WAS EXCRUCIATINGLY PAINFUL TO ME. THEN THERE WAS ANOTHER. I CHARGED FORWARD TO GET AWAY FROM THE NOISE, THE PAIN, BUT WHEN JUST A FEW STRIDES FORWARD, I COULD RUN NO MORE. I FELL TO MY KNEES AND FELT THE WARM, BUT UNFAMILIAR SENSATION OF BLOOD RUNNING FROM MY EAR. I'D BEEN SHOT. TWO BULLETS HAD ENTERED MY HEAD JUST BEHIND MY LEFT EAR. YEARS AGO SOME BAD BOYS HAD SHOT ME BUT IT DIDN'T HURT THEN AS IT DID NOW. THIS PAIN WAS ARRESTING TO MY HEART. I LIFTED MY CHIN AND LET OUT MY LAST RIGHTEOUS BELLOW OF PROTEST. THEN I FELL TO MY SIDE AND THE WEIGHT OF MY ORGANS SHIFTED. I COULD FEEL MY SOUL BEING GATHERED AND REORGANIZED AND KNEW THAT I WAS GOING. I DID NOT MIND, EXCEPT FOR THE SADNESS I ALREADY FELT IN LEAVING WILLIAM ALONE. HIS CRIES OF ANGUISH WERE LOUD IN MY HURTING EAR. I WRAPPED MY TRUNK AROUND HIM IN ONE LAST EMBRACE AND PURRED MY DEVOTION TO HIM. LEAVING WILLIAM WORRIED ME AND OF COURSE, THE CONCERN OF WHAT WOULD HAPPEN TO MY BONES WAS GREAT. I KNEW I COULD DO NOTHING ABOUT THAT. YEBO, IT WAS TIME FOR ME TO PASS.

THEN I WAS GONE FROM MY BODY, WHICH WILLIAM CONTINUED TO CRY OVER AND EMBRACE AND REMEMBER, JUST AS MY KIND DOES FOR EACH OTHER WHEN WE PASS AWAY IN OUR HOME LAND. PERHAPS THAT IS WHAT HIS KIND

DID FOR EACH OTHER TOO. I ONLY KNOW THAT IT IS NOT AT ALL WHAT MISTER BAILEY DID.

OH JESUS GOD, JESUS GOD, NO!

WHAT IS HAPPENING?

MISTER BAILEY? BETTE – YOU OKAY?

SHE BEEN SHOT MISTER BAILEY!

YOU GOT TO GET HER SOME HELP

LOOK SHE BLEEDIN BAD!

bette you jus rest easy now

he gone for help

get you a doctor maybe

please dont die bette

oh dear oh no

my best friend bette

***

she gone mister bailey she dead

we got to bury her

here by the road

lookin out over

that pretty pond

she'd like that

we got to mister bailey

send that doctor away

why he openin his bag

what you fixin to do

NO!

you cant be doin like that

mister bailey please dont do

what mister owen done

i seen that once

i cant see it again

punish me all you want

i wont help with that

i wont see that

I wont

again

We don't have any time to waste,
let's just get this job done.
Dang it, Will, you don't got to watch.
You just go get the shovel
and dig the dang hole
if burying her so important to you!
We'll do this job that's got to be done.
Couldn't bury her whole any way.
How you think we could move
five tons of dead elephant?

Where is the sheriff?
I want some answers!
Why would anybody want to kill
an ole elephant that never hurt nobody?
Everybody remember it's important
to get the skin and head off
as cleanly as possible.
I need all the big bones too.
We can wash 'em off in the pond
before loading up the wagon.
All the other parts – pile over here.
My man will bury that. The offal.
I'll pay a quarter to every man or boy
that helps with this job, God-awful.

All right, doc, tell us what to do.
Jesus, this is a terrible loss...

i fetched the shovel

ole monkey spit at me

i cussed him back

held the oak handle

in my bloody hands

wiped the dinged up spade

had a half a mind

to walk back there

an hit bailey with it

but i aint never been like that

i was jus all tore up

with sadness and anger

an such a bad feeling

of what happened to gaja

coming back to me

now i got double those feelings

its a heavy weight on you

when an elephant dies

mos folks know nothin of it

jus awful it is   now I got it

two times

i thought maybe

it best i jus run off

they was all busy

no one would be lookin for me

til they done cuttin her up

spreadin her out on the road

like you gut a fish for dinner

i stood there a while

thinkin on it

stood there not doin nothing

the thought that stuck with me was

maybe its jus time

for me to go

to walk away

theres no more elephants

for me to take care of

this is a place

where maybe

maybe i can

make my own way

in the world

those merry dancers

told me i'd be welcome

at their holy land

and theres indians

up in the woods

where a man can live free

some kind of way

that must be it

   but then i knew

if i dont stay

an see to her burial

   at least the parts

he aint going to haul away

theyd probably jus leave

   the rest of her

for the dogs and the crows

couldn't let that happen

if i dont dig the hole

aint no hole

going to get dug

   so i stayed

dug the dang hole

dug til my hands bled

   my back ached

but my back

wasnt the part of me

   hurtin most

I can't state plainly enough
that I want that man, that criminal,
brought to justice. Further I expect
to be reimbursed for my losses
which since I came to this town
have been egregiously high.
That elephant was worth
more than a thousand dollars!
And now my elephant keeper
has gone missing!
He's worth nearly that much.
My stop in your town
may just bankrupt me.

Yes, I'm sure.
His things are missing.
He's called William.
'Bout this tall, very dark.
I checked the wagon front to back.
His old blue coat, extra white shirt,
his little pouch, his porcupine basket,
all missing. That's all he had
and they're all gone
so I guess he's run off
'less you got another criminal
that stole him away.
Didn't take his horse.
He knows better than that.
He might come to his senses
when he's done grieving
the Elephant.

He gets very attached,
has a hard time when they die.
He may turn up after I'm gone.
If so, I'd appreciate if you
enact the law on my behalf.
Don't want him making
a pest of himself
as President Jefferson says
of free blacks set loose.

I'll be getting another elephant,
make no mistake about it.
I want him returned to me
in a state fit to work.
I thank you in advance
for your help with that.
Your town owes me
a favor or two.

Inmate David Daniels
Court of law at Alfred, Maine
1816

Yes, sir, I do fully understand
the charges made against me as read.
Yes sir, I plead not guilty,
for reasons of extenuating circumstances.
Yes sir, I would like to state my case.
Someone could just bring me a bible
                    to swear on first.

I, David Josiah Daniels, do
solemnly swear to tell the truth,
so help me God. First of all,
I keep hearing the word murder
                    getting tossed about.

That's just more nonsense of the kind
that people in this county been tossing
about these last years, to start strife
where there is no cause
                    to do so.

Tis true, I'd hit upon hard times.
My brother died, quite of a sudden,
left me holding a considerable debt
and two families to feed.
You being a judge and all, you
are certainly aware of the tax trouble,
                    your honor.

Sum told, I owe for this and that.
So they come around saying
they'd take my mill from me.
My father's grist mill, what's
served the people for near fifty years.
One hard year and you aim
to shut me down and sell her.
Aint right. Any reasonable man
                would say so.

The Elephant,
yes sir, I'm getting to it.
I got notice of the date they was fixing
to remove me from my property,
by force, they said,
                if necessary.

Well, I decided I might as well
drink the store of whiskey we'd put up,
so they wouldn't get that too.
Made from corn we ground ourselves,
super fine.
                It's an art, doing that.

Well, your honor, I'm sorry to say,
that by virtue of my melancholy
I drank too much of the stuff,
lost my mind
                for a period of time.

I've no memory of shooting an elephant
so can't confess to doing it.
I think you're likely to agree

that shooting an elephant is not
something a man is likely to forget doing
even if he's as fuddled as that elephant
                frequently was!

And it's my understanding that there isn't
anyone who can say he saw me do it.
I do confess to having
a whole head full of bad feelings about
        the Elephant.

All these people 'round here
can't scrape together one dang dollar
to pay the miller, never seem
to have trouble coming up with fifty cents
for every head in their household
to come to town to see an elephant
             drink itself stupid.

That elephant owner should be ashamed.
Paying twenty five cents to see
the Elephant
is a bad way to be taking money
out of the pockets of people
who needed it more. Worst of all
they're even willing to do it on Sundays.
No tithing. No Sir. Just got to go see
        the Elephant.

I'd say they's all sorts
of hypocrisy in that.
And one dead elephant.
Only like I said,

I can't rightly say
                I killed it.

And it's just an elephant
so you can't call it murder any more
than if a cow or horse is killed.
Could've been some kind of accident,
a misfire maybe.
                You can't prove otherwise.

Mister Thorndike, here's my address
in Somers, New York
so you can keep me posted.
Let us review the agreement
before we sign.

You agree to sail your ship,
the *Columbia*, to Calcutta,
and purchase an elephant
no more than five feet high
and in sound health.

The total amount you'll be paid
is not to exceed the sum
of 8000 dollars,
the balance of which
will be paid to you

upon receipt of an elephant
as afore mentioned
delivered at either
Boston or New York Harbor
within one year's time

commencing from the date
of your departure
from these shores.
God speed to you,
sir.

The New York Post
1817

<u>NOTICE</u>

The skeleton of

The Elephant

that was shot the 26th of July last

in District of Maine,

so well known by the public,

is got up for inspection

and may be seen at No. 301 Broadway

from Monday the 7th until Wednesday the 30th instant,

every day in the week, Sunday excepted

from nine in the morning until sunset

the weight of

The Elephant

when it was shot

was upwards of 70 hundred pounds.

Admittance 25 cents.

Hello Mother! Here, I have brought
a jar of huckleberry jam that
Mariah put up. I bring news too.
Mama, she is with child!
Due in six months' time.

Now, on to circus business.
Mariah will have to quit
her equestrian act, but
will continue showing the horses
but I have more news ...

do you remember years ago
we all helped make a big blanket
for wintering over
the Elephant
that Papa used to keep her covered?

From that we have designed
a big round top tent
that we can easily set up
in any place.

The show will be held under it.

No one will get to see
the Elephant
or anything else until they've paid.
It will keep off sun and rain.
It'll be held up by poles that
the Elephant
will set up and take down.

I've more announcements.
I think I should like to try at
being a clown.
I can dress silly
and cut up for folks.

And lastly, while on tour,
I found land in Fairfax County,
not far from the Federal City,
so many folks pass coming and going.
It's just perfect for our plans.
Yes, my buttons are a'bursting!
We are so very fortunate.
I will bring her this tea straightaway.
Please give my regards to all the family,
And the neighbors too.

I'd heard a circus was coming.

Traveled a couple of days

jus' to take a look.

Jus' thinking 'bout it give me

a mixed up set of feelings.

Some good, some bad, and

a lot somewhere in the middle.

I needed to know if the circus

had an elephant.

I wanted to know if it was

Bailey and Company's Splendid Circus.

Had to see for myself if they was

splendid without me and Bette.

Turned out to be a different circus.

Guess they's a lot of 'em now.

Folks jus' can't get enough

of seeing elephants.

Sure enough they had one.
I couldn't get too close
but got a good enough look
from afar.

First bull elephant I ever seen.
Huge Indian called Mogul.
Looked sad like the girls.
Maybe moreso

      as they was makin' him
wear silly clothes and do silly tricks
an elephant don't have no cause
nor want to do.

Never seen so many chains and whips
needed for jus' one creature. Never.
Couldn't bear to get closer
after what I seen from afar.

He had a broken spirit, was jus'
doin' things so not to get hurt.
Sure was being treated cruelly.
That's a word I know now.

Well, I always known it really.
That was all I could stand to see.
Couldn't look on it no more.
Jus' walked back into the dark

     of the pine trees.
Looked at the endless stand of 'em
goin' on forever.
     Wondered

did they serve me
     as cage or castle.
Not sure I know.
     Felt bad walking away
into the pines.
     Weren't nothing else
I could do,

and God knows

I had seen

the Elephant.

EPILOGUE

AHH, YOU THOUGHT WE WERE GONE, DIDN'T YOU? HA! ONE OF THE MANY SHORT COMINGS OF YOUR SPECIES, THE PROFOUND LACK OF UNDERSTANDING ABOUT LIFE. OUR PHYSICAL BODIES ARE GONE, YES OF COURSE. YOU KNOW HOW WE DIED. YOU KNOW WHAT YOUR PEOPLE DID TO OUR DEAD BODIES. SKINNED AND STUFFED US. SENT PIECES OF US HITHER AND YON. LIKE TROPHIES OR SOUVENIRS OR ITEMS OF STUDY FOR YOUR PEOPLE. OR WORSE YET, MAKING EVEN OUR REMAINS DO PARLOR TRICKS FOR THE ENTERTAINMENT OF YOUR OTHERS. A FATE THAT BEFELL MANY OF OUR KIND ALL OVER THE PLANET. DID YOU LEARN ANYTHING FROM THE STUDY OF OUR DEAD AND DUSTY SELVES? ANYTHING THAT WOULD ADVANCE YOUR CIVILIZATION? WE THINK NOT.

HOWEVER, THAT IS NOT THE BONE WE HAVE TO PICK WITH YOU. THE BONE WE HAVE TO PICK WITH YOU IS THE MATTER OF OUR BONES. DO YOU KNOW WHAT BECAME OF OUR BONES? ANY ONE OF YOU HAVE ANY IDEA?

THEREIN LIES THE PROBLEM. YOU DO NOT KNOW. YOU CANNOT KNOW. BECAUSE THE PEOPLE FROM WHOM YOU DESCEND DID NOT CARE. GAJA'S SACRED BONES ARE MISSING. THE VERY FIRST ELEPHANT IN THE UNITED STATES OF AMERICA. SOMETHING THE PEOPLE PURPORTED TO CARE ABOUT GREATLY AND BELIEVED TO BE IMPORTANT ENOUGH TO BRING HERE BECAME SO UNIMPORTANT THAT HER DEATH WENT UNRECORDED FOR POSTERITY. A CREATURE WHO GAVE HERSELF TO YOUR NATION. BUT WORSE THAN THAT IS THAT NO ONE KNOWS

WHAT BECAME OF HER SACRED BONES. YOUR NATION LOST THEIR VERY FIRST ELEPHANT. LOST HER. WITHOUT A TRACE. THE LARGEST LAND MAMMAL ON THE PLANET, AND A ONE-OF-A-KIND BEING. YOU LOST HER. YOU TALKED ENDLESSLY FOR DECADES ABOUT SEEING THE ELEPHANT, BUT NO ONE KNOWS WHERE SHE WAS LAST SEEN. HOW DOES A NATION OF PEOPLE WHO PRIDE THEMSELVES ON LEADERSHIP AND ENTERPRISE LOSE AN ELEPHANT? SHE MUST BE AROUND HERE SOMEWHERE. THERE IS AN ELEPHANT IN THE ROOM, IN THIS GREAT BIG ROOM YOU CALL THE UNITED STATES OF AMERICA, AND THOUGH HISTORY DID NOT BOTHER TO RECORD HER NAME SHE HAD ONE.

THEN THERE IS THE MATTER OF ME. I WAS GIVEN A NAME. SEVERAL ACTUALLY. YOU SEEM AS INCAPABLE OF KEEPING TRACK OF ELEPHANT NAMES AS YOU WERE OF THE ELEPHANTS THEMSELVES. OFTEN I WAS CALLED OLDE BETTE, THOUGH THAT IS PREPOSTEROUS AS LIKE GAJA, I DIED WHILE STILL QUITE YOUNG. SOMETIMES I WAS CALLED BIG BETTE, OR BETTY. I WAS MURDERED, WITHOUT CAUSE, AND, JUST LIKE GAJA, MY SKIN AND BONES WERE TAKEN IN A GRUESOME WAY AND PUT ON DISPLAY. OLD MAN BAILEY STILL PROFITING BY MY EXHIBITION, DRAGGING THE DEAD ME FROM PLACE TO PLACE. UNTIL AT LAST MY FLESH AND BONES WERE SOLD TO P. T. BARNUM, TO BE SHOWN FOR PROFIT, IN HIS LITTLE MUSEUM OF ODDITIES. SOME OF MY BONES LEFT HERE, SOME OF MY BONES LEFT THERE. NO ONE CARED ABOUT SPLITTING THEM UP. SELLING SOME. STEALING SOME. A WAYWARD DOG OR CURIOUS CHILD COULD DIG UP ONE OR TWO AGAIN WITH NO REGARD FOR WHAT IS SACRED. IT IS OFT CLAIMED THAT MY REMAINS WERE LOST TO A FIRE THAT CONSUMED BARNUM'S BUILDING, AND CREMATION IS AT LEAST, A MORE RESPECTFUL WAY TO TREAT SACRED REMAINS, THAN LOSING THEM ONLY GOD KNOWS WHERE. BUT WHAT YOUR PEOPLE FAIL TO GRASP IS THAT BONES DON'T BURN. NOT ENTIRELY, AND ESPECIALLY NOT BIG BONES SUCH AS MINE.

MOST OF MY MOST SACRED PARTS WERE STILL THERE SOMEWHERE WHEN YOUR FIRE WAS EXTINGUISHED IN A MESSY PILE OF CHARRED DEBRIS LIKE THAT I HELPED YOU WITH DURING ONE OF YOUR WARS. AND WHAT BECAME OF MY BONES? OLDE BETTE'S BIG BONES? THE SECOND ELEPHANT IN AMERICA. THE FIRST FROM AFRICA. WHO GAVE HERSELF TO YOUR PEOPLE. YOU HAVE LOST THEM TOO.

WE ARE UNITED, IN THIS PURGATORY OF WAITING AND WONDERING, WHERE HAVE OUR BONES BEEN STREWN ALL OVER YOUR GREAT SAVANNAH, AND HOW CAN THEY BE FOUND AGAIN, AND PUT TO REST PROPERLY, SO THAT WE CAN, FINALLY, REST. CAN YOU IMAGINE HOW IT FEELS TO BE UNABLE TO REST IN PEACE? CAN YOU IMAGINE IF YOUR REMAINS WERE STREWN ABOUT AND LOST?

ALSO QUITE DISTRESSING TO US, IS THAT YOU HAVE IN THE SAME MANNER OF SELFISHNESS, LOST THE REMAINS OF OUR BELOVED WILLIAM. THE ONE OF YOU WHO CARED FOR US EACH AND EVERY DAY. THE MAN WHO FED US AND BATHED US AND TAUGHT US AND CONSOLED US AND REWARDED US AND NURSED US AND PLAYED WITH US WHEN WE WERE LOST AND ALONE. TRULY LOST AND ALONE. THERE WAS WILLIAM. AND YOUR HISTORICAL RECORD TELLS LESS OF HIM THAN IT DOES OF US. HE TOO HAS DISAPPEARED. FROM YOUR RECORDS. FROM YOUR MEMORY. AND THAT TOO IS, SIMPLY, WRONG.

WE HAVE COME BACK ONLY TO TELL YOU THIS. THIS MESSAGE OF GRAVEST URGENCY THAT SHOULD NOT HAVE TO BE COMMUNICATED TO YOU AT ALL BECAUSE YOU SHOULD KNOW IT IN YOUR OWN BONES, WHERE ALL THE IMPORTANT KNOWLEDGE IS STORED. THE WISDOM OF YOUR MOTHERS, AND THEIR MOTHERS, AND SO ON. IT IS IN YOUR BONES.

BUT WE MUST SAY IT BECAUSE WE CANNOT, WILL NOT, REST IN PEACE UNTIL YOU FIND AND CONSECRATE OUR BONES. WE GAVE YOU OUR LIVES. PLEASE, YOU SHOULD GIVE US THIS. THE WAY THAT OUR LIVES SHOULD HAVE

BEEN HONORED WHEN WE PASSED. WE TRUST THAT YOU FINE YOUNG PEOPLE WILL RIGHT THIS WRONG, BRINGING HONOR BOTH TO US, AND TO YOURSELVES. AND PEACE. YOUR KIND NEEDS PEACE, AND THE WAY TO PEACE, THE ONLY WAY, IS TO MAKE WRONGS RIGHT. YOU CAN DO IT. WE HAVE ELEPHANTINE FAITH IN YOU, THE YOUNG ONES. BOTH OF US WERE DENIED THE GREAT INNATE DESIRE TO HAVE A BABY AND PERPETUATE OUR SPECIES. AND SO YOU ARE THE ONLY CHILDREN WE WILL EVER HAVE. WE FEEL A MATERNAL FONDNESS FOR YOU, AND BELIEVE THAT YOU WILL HELP US.

DON'T THINK THAT YOU MUST DO IT TO EARN FORGIVENESS. WE HAVE ALREADY FORGIVEN YOU, AND ALL THOSE THAT CAME BEFORE YOU, FOR COMPASSION AND KINDNESS IS OUR WAY. WE ASK THAT YOU DO IT FOR YOU. THE TIME HAS COME FOR THAT.

THE TIME TO DO IT IS NOW. THE ONE TO DO IT IS YOU. PLEASE, WE IMPLORE YOU, TRY TO FIND OUR BONES AND MAKE THEM SACRED. IT CAN BE DONE. IF YOU TRY AND FAIL THAT WILL BE FINE. IF YOU LOOK WITHIN AND FIND THAT YOU CANNOT TRY, THAT WILL BE FINE TOO. PERHAPS YOU WILL COME TO SERVE A HIGHER PURPOSE. OR PERHAPS YOU WILL HOLD IN YOUR HAND SOMEDAY THE LIFE OF ANOTHER, A CREATURE THAT MAY BE GREAT IN SIZE AND STATURE OR MEEK AND MILD, AND YOU WILL CHOOSE TO TREAT THAT CREATURE THE WAY YOU WOULD LIKE TO BE TREATED. PERHAPS THERE IS NO HIGHER PURPOSE THAN THAT.

ONLY HAVE A RELATIONSHIP WITH ANOTHER LIVING BEING FOR THE GIFTS THAT COME FROM FRIENDSHIP, WHICH CANNOT BE FORESEEN. DO NOT ENTER INTO A RELATIONSHIP WITH ANOTHER FOR WHAT YOU CAN GET FROM THAT CREATURE. LIKEWISE NEVER ASK ANOTHER TO GIVE UP THEIR DIGNITY FOR YOU. NEVER. THINK OF IT AS THE ULTIMATE ELEPHANT TEST; IT CANNOT BE DESCRIBED, BUT YOU WILL KNOW IT WHEN YOU COME UPON IT.

AND YOU WILL COME UPON IT. YOU WILL, SOMEWHERE ALONG YOUR PATH.

WHATEVER PATH YOU CHOOSE, WHATEVER CHOICE YOU MAKE - JUST REMEMBER. DO NOT FORGET WHO WAS HERE AND HOW THEY SERVED THIS LIFE. MEMORY IS SACRED TOO.

IN ADVANCE, WE SAY NAMASTE, AND REMAIN, ALWAYS, YOUR OBEDIENT AND LOYAL FRIENDS,

GAJA AND BIG BETTE

A Note from the Author

In *For to See the Elephant* I have tried to tell a realistic story of American history, particularly the story of the very first elephants to arrive in the United States, who each came alone and spent all of their remaining years here, the rest of their shortened lives, without ever seeing another of their own kind. Few good solid facts about their lives have survived, and all those I have found credible are included here. Most of the information available to us now is incredible for a variety of reasons including poor journalism and a lack of record keeping. Much of the information that we do have to work with is folk lore, or what might now be called urban legends. For all of those reasons it has become impossible to separate fact from fiction. So this is a fictional story based on facts. These really were the first two elephants to be here. Some of their story as told here is factual and much of it is fiction, informed by a considerable amount of research. This is how I imagined that it happened.

Most of the people were real, but not all of them. With the exception of his name, I created the character of William. I did that because I think he really existed but there is no record about him.

Nothing, absolutely nothing, is known about the fate of Gaja, who was unnamed or referred to as The Elephant, or Crowninshield's Elephant. Both she and Mister Owen disappear from the historical record, so I borrowed the relatively well documented death of Horatio the elephant who died as described in Westmoreland, New Hampshire in 1820 traveling with a different owner and black man. Big Bette's death happened very much as it is written of here. There was a Shaker Village in Maine (at the time they were called Merry Dancers by their neighbors) who were involved in abolition early on. Their involvement in any way with the elephant story is entirely fictional. Princess Sarah Molasses was a real Native girl living in Maine at the time but her seeing the elephant is entirely fictional, and the same is true of Ona Judge Staines of Portsmouth. Captain Nathaniel Hathorne and his log book were real, and his son Nathaniel would grow up and change the spelling of his name to Hawthorn and become the famous writer, but Junior's involvement with the elephant is entirely fictional. The Bailey family included all of the members I have written of but of course, as with all of the characters, I have invented their thoughts and words, and most of their actions.

I felt it was important to a realistic telling of the story to use eye witness or real newspaper accounts as often as possible to give an authentic context to the story. All of the diaries mentioning the elephant that I could find I have included as eye witness accounts. The diarists were Mister Hathorne, Mister John Davis, Reverend Bentley and the Quaker woman named Mrs. Drinker. It is important to remember that they all saw the elephant from their own point of view and a very different point in time. In the found poems the meaning of the original text has not been significantly altered.

Discussion Questions

1. Do you think it was right or wrong that the elephants were brought to the United States? Why or why not?
2. Could it have been done differently? What would you do differently if you were one of the men involved?
3. Is William's life as an enslaved man portrayed in this story in a way different from what most enslaved people would have endured? What are some consequences of slavery that he would have been likely to have suffered that are not covered in the story? What are some consequences of slavery to his life that are included in the story?
4. What do you think happened to William? What do you hope happened to William? If you could (and you can) write a new ending for his story what would it be?
5. The gender roles for boys and girls and men and women during the years of 1795 to 1825 were rigidly prescribed by society. In what ways did that show up in this story?
6. Which character in the story did you most identify with? Why? If you could speak to that character what would you say?
7. Which character in the story did you like the least? Why? If you could speak to that character what would you say?
8. What questions did the story leave you with that you would like to have answered?
9. In this story I have tried to give you an idea of what living in America in the early nineteenth century would have been like. What surprised you about life then? In what ways is your life different? Would you like to have lived during that time period? Why or why not?
10. Examine what your reactions were when an elephant was mistreated and when a person of color was mistreated. How were your reactions to each different and how can those differences be explained?

11. It has been said that the history of the elephant in America mirrors the growth of the nation over time. Can you draw any similarities between the two?
12. Do you think that it matters what happens to animal remains after their death? Or to human remains? Explain your position.
13. Do you understand the idiom "to see the elephant" now? How does the history of the idiom itself reflect the history of the elephant in America?
14. How many other elephant idioms did you find in the story? Can you determine what they mean by the context in which they are used? Can you determine how they originally came into being?

Acknowledgments

A writer is always indebted to many. For a writer of historical stories, some of those will be people long gone. I acknowledge them all and remain indebted to them, but hope remembering them provides some satisfaction. I also thank Dr. Richard Candee and research librarian Carolyn Marvin of the Portsmouth Athenaeum and librarian Mary Thompson of Mount Vernon, and the many friends and strangers who helped me shape this story into what it is today.

These adult books were among my primary sources:

The Tragedy of the Seas; Or, Sorrow on the Ocean, Lake, and River From Shipwreck, Plague, Fire and Famine by Charles Ellms. 1841.

Entertaining Elephants: Animal Agency and the Business of the American Circus by Susan Nance. John Hopkins University Press. 2013.

Behemoth: The History of the Elephant in America by Ronald Tobias. Harper Perennial. 2013.

Travels of John Davis in the United States of America (v.2): 1798 to 1802 by John Davis. 1803.

The Monthly Traveller, Or, Spirit of the Periodical Press. (periodical). 1835.

For a Short Time Only: Itinerants and the Resurgence of Popular Culture in Early America by Peter Benes. University of Massachusetts Press. 2016.

www.ingramcontent.com/pod-product-compliance
Lightning Source LLC
LaVergne TN
LVHW011155080426
835508LV00007B/410